ECONOMICS, TOWN PLANNING
AND TRAFFIC

Economics, Town Planning and Traffic

D. J. REYNOLDS

Published by
THE INSTITUTE OF ECONOMIC AFFAIRS
1966

FIRST PUBLISHED IN GREAT BRITAIN 1966 BY
THE INSTITUTE OF ECONOMIC AFFAIRS LIMITED
EATON HOUSE
66A EATON SQUARE
LONDON SWI

PRINTED IN GREAT BRITAIN BY
IMPRESS (WORCESTER) LIMITED, HYLTON ROAD, WORCESTER

CONTENTS

Chapter

The nature of economics and the economy—Environmental wants—The scarcity of resources—The role of
economics in planning—Cost-benefit analysis—Economics, money and prices—Conclusions

The location of industry and industrial trends—An
optimum policy for industrial development—Industrial
redeployment—Poor prospects for development areas—
Housing trends—Green belts and other planning controls—
Imperfection and control in the housing market—Transport and road pricing—Road costs, congestion and
pricing—Rail—the subsidised commuter—Town planning
and rational transport pricing policies—No public
assistance for the private motorist

v

TABLES

FIGURES

PREFACE

THE INCREASING attention in recent public debate to town planning and regional development has been mainly provoked by the mounting problems of housing shortages, 'declining' areas, rising rates, road congestion and unsatisfactory public transport. The atmosphere of crisis in which the debate is customarily conducted has been fomented by the failure of post-war governments to show the political will or the economic understanding required for practical reforms. Their advisers—sociologists, town planners, administrators and others—have concentrated on utopian solutions which for all their grandeur are only loosely related to the capacity of the economy to finance them. And current planning studies with vague or inconsistent methods, and objectives unrelated to costs or demands, may be obscuring rather than clarifying the approach to rational policy.

In this situation the Institute thought it would be helpful to publish an economic study of town planning in terms of limited resources and their allocation to alternative uses by reference to their costs and consumers' valuations of their services. Mr D. J. Reynolds, a noted transport economist who has also studied and worked on town planning and the distribution of industry for some 17 years, has compiled a major survey that should enlighten economists by its application to town planning and town planners by its economic analysis. Not least, its sceptical approach should call a timely halt to the divorce between the technical proposals of enthusiasts and economic realities.[1]

---

[1] In reporting the British Sociological Association conference on 'Urbanism in Contemporary Britain', *New Society* (7 April, 1966) commented: 'The town planners want answers or say they do: the sociologists want to give these answers. The snag is that all too often the techniques of sociology are still too crude for the purpose. The gap between accumulated fact and general theory seems wide.'

Previous IEA publications have touched on aspects of the central subject-matter discussed by Mr Reynolds. In *Hobart Papers* Mr Norman Macrae,[1] Mr John Carmichael[2] and Dr D. R. Denman[3] have documented the failure of government policies in the markets for housing and land. Mr John Hibbs[4] has criticised the institutional and legal framework in which public bus transport operates and has advocated a return to competition and reform of passenger transport licensing. Mr Gabriel Roth[5] has outlined a scheme for pricing the use of scarce road space that would serve the dual purpose of rationing it and raising finance for its expansion. The characteristics which these authors have in common have been their practical approach to economic policy and the application of micro-economic analysis to markets for individual goods and services. This approach is demonstrated by Mr Reynolds, originally a Buchanan enthusiast and adherent of the macro-economic, long-run planning attitude to the 'town of the future', whose researches and practical experience have persuaded him that urban renewal and town planning must rest on economic first principles.

Mr Reynolds's emphasis is upon the inescapable logic of scarcity. Chapter I outlines the role of markets and prices and draws the conclusion that it is not within the power of the Treasury to conjure resources into existence for what is only one among many competing projects by a stroke of the governmental pen.[6] The clamour by teachers, doctors, pensioners and others for a larger share of government revenue, and the evident difficulty of raising much more than 40 per cent of national income in taxation is enforcing attention to new solutions to old problems.

Chapters 2 and 3 comprise a critical analysis of the background trends and policies in the distribution of industry, housing, transport, planning controls and land values. Chapters 4 and 5 analyse the Buchanan Report, *Traffic in Towns*, and raise serious doubts.

---

[1] *To Let*, Hobart Paper 2, IEA, 1960.

[2] *Vacant Possession*, Hobart Paper 28, IEA, 1964.

[3] *Land in the Market*, Hobart Paper 30, IEA, 1964.

[4] *Transport for Passengers*, Hobart Paper 23, IEA, 1963.

[5] *A Self-Financing Road System*, Research Monograph 3, IEA, 1966.

[6] 'The Treasury's allocations are *hopelessly* inadequate—though the philosophy of *Traffic in Towns* seems to have been accepted, the thinking about investment has not moved forward one inch.' Colin Buchanan, Letter to *The Times*, 23 March, 1966.

Mr Reynolds argues not only that its proposals could be implemented only in the long term on the most optimistic assumptions concerning the availability of resources, but also that, even if they were feasible, one of its fundamental assumptions—that we should retain our towns in broadly their present form—could be called in question. He contends that the Buchanan approach overestimated the likelihood of 'intolerable' congestion and failed to appreciate the relevance of road pricing, which would avoid the necessity for the arbitrary and unworkable distinction between 'optional' and 'essential' traffic. Mr Reynolds argues that road pricing would have three further merits: it would encourage dispersal of the central attractors that help to cause congestion, offer a more reliable method than cost-benefit accounting[1] of deciding where resources could most profitably be invested, and reduce the area of arbitrariness in town planning decisions.

For Mr Reynolds the third merit of road pricing is crucial, since he maintains that the current scope and complexity of town planning as it is developing are going far beyond the point at which planners can know what they are doing. These decisions would be simplified if they were guided by a framework of markets and prices. He thus traces the arbitrariness of planning policy to the absence or imperfections of markets for housing, land, roads, transport and other (mostly public) services. More attention to economic problems and the improvement of charging policies for housing, roads, and gas, water and electricity connections would reduce reliance on fallible forecasts and over-ambitious long-term plans.

In Chapter 6 Mr Reynolds attempts a planner's analysis of the demand for housing on the assumption that the distortions and imperfections will not be removed and that the influence of government on demand and the house-building industry will remain dominant. For all its technical dexterity Mr Reynolds remains unconvinced of the reliability of long-term planning and therefore of the fundamental value of forecasting. His experiences in the Treasury and later as a town planning economist have persuaded him of the unlikelihood of state action directing resources efficiently to

[1] For a critical appraisal of the merits and deficiencies of this technique see G. H. Peters, *Cost-Benefit Analysis and Public Expenditure*, Eaton Paper 8, IEA, 1966.

satisfy individual preferences. He concludes that if market prices were made the determinants of economic choices and the problems of town planning thereby simplified, the planner would be freed to undertake the regulatory and design functions which are his chief strengths and for which he is best equipped.

Mr Reynolds's thesis is thus very relevant to the major socio-economic question raised by the 'attenuation of private property rights' which has been a characteristic of the development of town planning over the past 100 years: how far can town planning in the social interest be taken in a mixed economy and remain consistent with the working of the market?[1] It may be that it has already gone too far: for in the absence of markets it is difficult to relate the use of scarce resources closely to the preferences of consumers from whom alone the final valuation of output can derive.

Chapters 7 and 8 develop Mr Reynolds's detailed alternatives both to current policy and to the Buchanan proposals. Concentrations of urban population should be dispersed ('the argument that Britain is overcrowded and *therefore* that we should live at higher densities is not the self-evident truth it is sometimes held to be'[2]); pricing should be applied to roads; ring roads should be built; and we may be able towards the end of the century to consider the construction of central road grids and a more refined conception of Professor Buchanan's 'environmental areas'. Population increase, the author argues, and recent Ministry of Housing studies have confirmed, will be more economically accommodated in new rather than expanded towns.

In conclusion Mr Reynolds restates his case against the conception of town planning as the 'grand design' and advocates as 'only just worthwhile' more modest, short-term planning guided by markets and prices within a 40-year 'rolling' plan, the prime object of which is to anticipate difficulties. Even here there are problems: as Mr John Brunner has argued,[3] a 'rolling plan' is a confession that planning has failed, for if the plan follows on the

---

[1] See H. Ronald Parker, 'The History of Compensation and Betterment since 1900', *Land Values*, ed. Peter Hall, Sweet and Maxwell, 1965.
[2] Page 59.
[3] *The National Plan: a preliminary assessment*, Eaton Paper 4, second edition, July 1965, pp.38—9.

heels of events what is its point in the first place? The general
case against policies based upon collective long-term forecasts is that
they assume a given set of conditions will occur. But such
assumptions are prone to error. Our ignorance of the future increases
with the length of the period to which the forecast relates, the
complexity of the phenomena under consideration and the degree
of specificity of the prediction. (It would be easier to say that car
sales will rise than to forecast which firm will sell most.) Though
Mr Reynolds does not discuss the general problem, his position is
clear: 'We only have the resources to transform our towns and cities
substantially over a long period and cannot foresee the future
accurately. Therefore the function of comprehensive planning must
be . . . modest.'[1] He urges further research into road pricing, which
he prefers to a payroll tax as a method of dispersal, and invites
town planners to accept economic analysis as a means of simplifying
their task.

Mr Reynolds's survey will be welcomed by economists, sociologists, town planners and others for its detailed analysis and
perceptive comment. There will not be universal agreement with
his conclusions but there can be little doubt of the value of his
study in concentrating attention upon the contribution that economists can make to the formation of opinion and policy on the
recalcitrant problems of urban planning and development. Pre-
occupation with technical means and ends has bedevilled much
thinking and writing on town planning; town planners like Dr
Nathaniel Lichfield have seen the imperative need to introduce
economics into the discussion of town planning. Mr Reynolds's
book is virtually the first to do so in Britain at least.

We are grateful to Mr F. G. Pennance, head of the department of
economics at the College of Estate Management, Mr G. J. Ponsonby,
formerly Reader in Transport in the University of London, and
Mr Ralph Turvey, of the Central Electricity Generating Board,
for comments and criticism on early drafts. The Institute and
members of the Advisory Council do not necessarily accept the
author's argument or conclusions, but the Institute offers them
as a stimulating contribution to public understanding of a subject
that has for too long remained divorced from economic analysis.

August 1966   IEA

[1] Page 140.

THE AUTHOR

D. J. REYNOLDS was educated at Wallingford Grammar School, Berks., and at Exeter University (then a University College) graduating in economics in 1949. After working on distribution of industry and associated planning problems in the Board of Trade from 1949 to 1953, he studied the economics of roads and road transport at the Road Research Laboratory until 1961. Following a period of research on the economics of transport in Ireland, he has been analysing the economic aspects of urban traffic and planning, and is currently employed by a firm of consultants working on these problems.

ACKNOWLEDGEMENTS

MY THANKS for comments, criticisms and suggestions on early drafts of this book are due to Dr P. A. Stone of the National Institute of Economic and Social Research, Mr R. Thomas of the Greater London Council, Mr G. J. Roth, the transport economist, and Mr J. M. Thomson, Research Fellow in Transport at the London School of Economics. The final responsibility for the views and conclusions expressed is however entirely my own; they are not necessarily those of any organisation with which I am or have been connected.

D. J. R.

INTRODUCTION

IT IS surprising that until recently little interest has been taken by town planners in economics and by economists in planning[1] in Britain; for whether planning is regarded as a replacement of 'economic forces' as expressed by buyers and sellers in the market for urban development or as part of the legal and institutional framework created for the market, it is of concern to both disciplines that it should be well-conceived and effective.

There is no obvious reason for this lack of interest of economists in planning beyond the tendency to separate academic disciplines in Britain, although economists have shown considerable interest over a long period in land values and their taxation. But a relatively simple explanation for the comparative lack of interest of planners in economics lies in the historical origins of planning with its emphasis on the aesthetic. Planning was designed to interfere with 'economic forces' when they produced results out of harmony with the planner's aesthetic intuition, so that there was a tendency to regard economics itself as a force to be resisted rather than as an intellectual discipline to be used as part of the planner's basic equipment. Finally, the planner's scepticism has been reinforced by a common misunderstanding of the nature of economics—to regard it merely as a narrow form of arithmetic used in the calculation of costs rather than as a systematic method for the allocation of resources and choice between alternative uses of which money-cost calculations are merely a by-product.

For various reasons, therefore, town planners have tended to look upon economics with some disfavour, despite the contributions that the economist can make to their work. Economics is concerned with the allocation of scarce resources between compe-

[1] Throughout the book the word 'planning' refers to town planning unless otherwise indicated.

I

ting uses and wants, and normally (but not exclusively) economists study the market and the price mechanism; demands of consumers in the market are reflected via the price mechanism back through distribution and production, and in this way final outputs of commodities are determined and productive resources allocated semi-automatically, in response to consumers' demands.[1]

At one period it was widely held that, with minimal interference by government, the free operation of the price system would result in the best allocation of resources and the maximisation of total welfare, though of course economists have always recognised the need for a legal and institutional framework to encourage competition among producers and harness private profit to public service.[2] But this ideal is deficient in some respects and intervention may be considered justifiable and often essential. We may adduce five reasons why town planning and other central actions may be called in aid to regulate the quantity and distribution of output that would be produced by a market system.

First, people's demands are obviously dependent on their incomes and capital and it can hardly be held that the distribution of income without intervention would be ideal. The state therefore tries to influence the distribution of income by taxation and subsidies, or more controversially, by physical provision in kind for no direct charge (as with the NHS) or at prices below market prices (as with publicly-provided housing).

Secondly, the differences between the private and public effects of some individual actions are such that state intervention and control is considered desirable. Thirdly, markets for some commodities such as roads and open spaces have been thought difficult or impossible to arrange, so that government has customarily undertaken their provision. (Sometimes government has provided services for which markets could have been arranged: government provision and market arrangement are often competing alternatives.[3]) Fourthly, a reason of rapidly increasing importance, the problems of harm-

---

[1] For a fuller explanation of the nature of economics for the non-economist, see Chapter 1.

[2] Lionel Robbins, *The Theory of Economic Policy in English Classical Political Economy*, Macmillan, 1952.

[3] For instance it is possible to charge motorists for the use of road space. See Chapter 2.

onising the components and effects of physical lay-out (buildings, roads and traffic) require some over-riding control or guidance. Finally, it is necessary to look ahead to anticipate problems and their solutions even though precise forecasts are impossible.

Nevertheless, it is a fallacy to suppose that economic analysis is therefore irrelevant to town planning. The price system still remains the major method of allocation of resources in our economy within whatever framework is devised for it, and such are the problems in planning that the market must remain an important allocative mechanism and indicator of preferences. Without pricing these problems can become fearsome. We should therefore welcome the work done by economists in trying to improve the market system as a method of allocation. The issue is therefore not whether economists ought or ought not to be for town planning, or town planners for or against economics, but whether the measures to be used are to supplement and assist the market or to distort it or put central direction in its place.[1]

Economics and town planning

Economics is of relevance and assistance to town planning in several ways. In the first place, the economic system is a means of expressing the wants of consumers and reconciling them with the scarcity of resources available for their satisfaction. Economic theory provides a system of reference, a discipline relating the particular to the general and the means of checking over-ambitious plans for which resources cannot rationally be made available. With vague and ambitious criteria it is hardly surprising that the Treasury is often obliged to say 'no', and that the planner is frustrated by the refusal.

In the second place, economics can help to provide a more quantitative and logical context for the formidable problems encountered in planning, either in its concepts (for example the much-discussed divergences between private and 'social' costs and the use of the price system to rectify them) or in the valuation of relevant variables as when market prices are used to determine the most efficient allocation of scarce resources. Finally, by taking fuller account of economic analysis planning ideas are more likely

[1] A simple discussion of this central issue from one who favours the market-oriented approach is in F. A. Hayek, *The Constitution of Liberty*, Routledge and Kegan Paul, 1960, Chapter 22.

to be acceptable to those responsible for allocating resources to them.

In a work of this kind it is necessary to specify an objective no matter how ambitious it may be. My aim has been to apply economics to the problems of the physical environment now and in the future (as far as it can be foreseen) so as to maximise human welfare. An immediate consequence of this aim is that all valuations are ultimately expressed in terms of human preferences and choices rather than by vaguer and more mystical ideas of value, of which the most frequently encountered is 'the public interest'.

Although this object emphasises the importance of economics in planning, it is not therefore suggested that economic efficiency is the end of all human endeavour. The highest goal must be conceived as something like human welfare, or the 'good life'. Economics is merely a means by which it may be achieved; it is not itself an end. Economic growth, affluence and its concomitants, which should make the 'good life' increasingly attainable, may paradoxically produce an unsatisfactory environment and reduce the amenities that people are striving to attain. This is one of the *raisons d'être* of town planning.

Nor should attention to economic analysis deter the desire and enthusiasm of the planner and the architect from seeking to create more beautiful and satisfying surroundings. Economics, aiming at objectivity, can have little to contribute to more subjective matters like aesthetics; it can however provide an analytical framework around which aesthetic decisions can be taken, thus enhancing rather than diminishing the probability of implementing them.

In this work four main problems predominate: the general one of securing a satisfying environment in an increasingly wealthy society (in which regional imbalance and questions of the urban/rural balance are dominant); the adaptation of our towns and cities to the car; methods of urban renewal; and the accommodation of the expected future increase in urban population. As will become clear, these problems are so formidable, and knowledge and data so rapidly changing, that this book can be claimed as no more than a contribution to its subject. In particular, starting from the immediate and down-to-earth problems of planning, it analyses them somewhat more deeply than is normal and attempts to cover the ground between the practical and the academic approaches. Although it is hoped that the advantages of tackling the problems in this way will become clear, in such a wide-ranging subject as planning the risks of falling between several stools can never be entirely absent.

One final word is necessary in introduction. It would be easy, popular, and fashionable to write a gentle book on planning which only discussed the problems and only tried to be 'constructive', but such a book would be of little value to planning which urgently needs contact with economic realities and criticism of alternative approaches. This view is not a matter of political or personal preference, for in the author's opinion there has been little to choose between the main political parties in their attitudes to planning in recent years. This book is the result of trying to apply economics to traffic, planning and related problems for some 17 years and of a growing realisation that economics must be the thread on which these matters must be strung to reduce them to order, consistency and reality. One may respect and sympathise with the aims of planning, but unless the plans are related to people's wants and the economy's resources, they will not meet the claims which are made for them and will, more often than not, never be realised.

CHAPTER I

THE NATURE OF ECONOMICS AND ITS APPLICATION TO TOWN PLANNING

'Economics is the science which studies human behaviour as a relationship between ends and scarce means which have alternative uses.' LORD ROBBINS.[1]

ECONOMISTS HAVE not always been good at explaining themselves to others. Perhaps that is why comment and criticism of economics and economists in planning and transport too often betray a misunderstanding of economics, its limitations and the contribution it can make towards securing the efficient provision and allocation of resources for road investment and other environmental improvements. It is therefore the more important to take issue with the notion, widely believed, that by a stroke of a pen at the Treasury or by some other administrative or financial device, resources can readily be provided for all 'socially essential' projects. And people appear to think that economics is solely concerned with finance and £ s d, in a way entirely set apart from people's personal, social and aesthetic lives, and that it promotes very different objectives to those of planners trying to secure an efficient and satisfying environment.[2]

Such misunderstanding is serious because, given the growing influence of economics, economic planning and the decision-making power of the Treasury, the case for road investment and improving the environment will go by default unless it is clearly established in economic terms. It may perhaps be thought that government can be pressed into more road investment by sheer

[1] *An Essay on the Nature and Significance of Economic Science*, Macmillan, 1932, p. 15.
[2] 'Buchanan Answers His Critics', *Architects Journal*, 16 June, 1965.

weight of lobbying, but government has many other problems to worry about.[1] Moreover political pressure is hardly a rational method of allocating scarce resources.

There is no doubt that the main onus for rectifying this regrettable state of affairs lies with the economist. For there are pitfalls and paradoxes in the subject and any specialist has a responsibility to explain himself both to other associated specialists and to the layman.

The nature of economics and the economy

It is difficult to explain the nature, extent and limitations of economics to the non-economist in a way that is both non-controversial and clear, yet acceptable to economic opinion. With this proviso, however, the starting point (and ultimate goal) in economics is with the individual and his wants. His wants remain subjective and personal until he commits resources to their satisfaction in terms of his time, property or effort. For this reason communal goals do not easily find a place in economics. The individual remains the only social unit capable of feeling pleasure and displeasure: because his requirements are diverse, and conflict with those of other people, subjective individual valuations do not permit the establishment of common goals.[2]

Usually the economist respects the individual's wants and preferences and takes them as given. He does not inquire into the motives or values behind them. People may have 'good' or 'bad' taste, but the evaluation of these questions is a matter for the moralist, educationist or aesthete, not for the economist *per se*; he may have his own views, but will not feel entitled to claim professional authority for them. Similarly the terms 'essential', 'necessity' or 'need' have little precise meaning in economics (certainly at our present standards of living), for economists are professionally concerned with competing uses to which resources may be put. If the provision of an 'essential' service involves the sacrifice of another 'essential' service, how is one to decide between them? They immediately raise the question 'essential for what?' with the further question whether the 'what' is essential. For example, it is

[1] *Public Expenditure 1963-4 to 1967-8*, Cmnd.2235, HMSO, 1963.
[2] Except for instance in time of war when the threat to the safety of all individuals may be held to establish the collective goal of winning the war.

often held that commercial vehicle trips are 'essential', but how 'essential' is it in the long run that a particular commercial trip takes place between that origin and that destination?

The individual's wants in primitive societies remain largely personal and subjective, and he satisfies them as best he can with the limited resources at his disposal. In more advanced societies wants are generally best and most productively satisfied by organisation, specialisation and exchange. That is to say, the individual finds it worthwhile to specialise and sell his labour (or other productive resources) for a common medium of exchange, money, and use this income to satisfy those of his wants that can be satisfied by specialisation, production and exchange.

The economic system based on voluntary exchange in markets gives an objective measure of his subjective values. Assuming that the individual—the consumer—spends his income so as to maximise his satisfaction from it, we can say that if he regularly spends, say, £1 on a unit of a commodity, he values a unit of that commodity at £1. Further we can say, but with less confidence, that if the demand and output of the commodity are increased by 1,000 units, valued at £1 per unit, with no extra effort, and all prices and all other outputs stay the same, the individuals comprising the community have gained by an amount valued at £1,000. But summing individual values is meaningful only if all people value a unit of income equally, and we cannot know whether or not they do. The significance of the market sector is that over a wide area of human wants there is a self-regulating, semi-automatic mechanism of allocation and decision-making which gives an objective measure of subjective values.[1] This system is *not* perfect and it is *not* universal but, as will be seen, it is difficult to create an equally efficient systematic mechanism for the valuation of output in those sectors of the economy where markets do not operate.

Environmental wants
In addition to purely subjective wants and those that can be met by the market system we have a penumbra of wants which are subjective in origin, cannot be met by the market system, yet which have wide social effects. Such wants are mainly aesthetic,[2] the desire for

[1] See pp. 14—15.
[2] Except for paintings and other *objets d'art* for which markets exist.

space, the countryside, etc., which are best summed up by Professor Buchanan's term 'the environment'.

Here the function of the economist is to point out the objective costs of preserving or improving the environment. But this does not mean that he is hostile to such aims, nor that he is unable to contribute to their advancement. He is only concerned to emphasise that the allocation of resources to one use implies a sacrifice of their contribution to all other possible uses.

Finally we have the wants that are satisfied by the public sector of the economy, consisting of government and defence, measures to redistribute income, and goods and services like roads, education, housing and health, which *could* be supplied by the private sector but which for varying reasons it has been politically decided should be provided by local or national government.

At present the public sector absorbs something like 40 per cent of the gross national product. Its *modus operandi* is that resources are withheld from private use by taxation and allocated by government, with no necessary correspondence between taxation of a particular commodity and public provision of a related service. Formally taxation is levied and public expenditure allocated politically. But this conventional statement of the decision-making process behind the allocation of public expenditure is over-simplified and incomplete, not least because it conceals the complex process by which governmental decisions are reached.[1] How this system works in detail and on what criteria is something of a mystery, certainly to the outsider; the main centres of decision lie within the Cabinet and the Treasury with the electorate accepting, tolerating or rejecting the outcome. Here the rôle of the economist is to advise on taxation, distribution of income, etc., and, more important, to attempt the Herculean task of devising relationships between costs and benefits of competing government expenditures, the products of which will not normally be valued in markets, as an aid to decision-making and the efficient allocation of resources.[2]

---

[1] For a discussion of some theoretical aspects of the centralised allocation of resources see J. M. Buchanan and Gordon Tullock, *The Calculus of Consent*, University of Michigan Press, 1962, and J. M. Buchanan, *The Inconsistencies of the National Health Service*, Occasional Paper 7, IEA, 1965.

[2] See below, p.12.

The scarcity of resources

Another central aspect of economics is that though man's wants are apparently limitless (but presumably of diminishing importance as they are progressively satisfied), the resources for their satisfaction are not. Therefore with full employment and a given state of technology, skill, effort, etc., *for the whole economy* it is not possible to obtain an increase in one form of output except at the expense of another. Assuming full employment of the nation's resources there is therefore no economic or financial device which will enable us to get something for nothing at any particular time. In the longer run technical and economic progress will give us a bonus in the form of an increase in national output. For this however there will be many claimants.[1]

This emphasis on the scarcity of resources in setting limits to the plans of enthusiasts has probably been responsible for much misunderstanding between the economist and other specialists, and for accusations of the dismal science. Yet the economist is not responsible for the scarcity of resources—the messenger must not be held responsible for the news he brings. Indeed he may assist in making scarce resources go further in meeting the almost limitless demands that are made upon them.

The rôle of economics in planning

The rôle apparently assigned to economics and to the economist in town planning, apart from their function as interpreters of general trends and relevant information, is to carry out cost-benefit studies on final plans and proposals in order to help in selecting the most worthwhile among alternative investments and policies. Economic and cost-benefit analyses are currently 'tacked on' to planning rather than integrated with it.

However this limited rôle is insufficient because, although cost-benefit studies may be appropriate to specific proposals such as that for the Victoria Line in London[2] or the best location for a

[1] For example, road investment involves the sacrifice of other things at the time it is made: thus a decision to invest £1 million requires the *simultaneous* diversion of equivalent resources from alternative uses, whether voluntarily by saving and borrowing or compulsorily by taxation.

[2] C. D. Foster and M. E. Beesley, 'Estimating the Social Benefits of Constructing an Underground Railway in London', *Journal of the Royal Statistical Society*, Vol. 126, Part 1, 1963.

particular development (other things assumed to stay equal), the alternatives in the overall town planning problem are so wide that the economist has a large prior rôle in helping to narrow down the options and to keep studies in touch with economic reality. Few towns or cities can be regarded as independent and self-contained from the planning point of view, so that planning must cover a wide range of factors and disciplines, and many alternative solutions to particular problems are possible. The prior rôle of the economist in comprehensive urban planning is therefore to contribute, *in conjunction with other disciplines*, a consistent standard of analysis and comparison throughout the planning process. It is doubtful whether there can be a useful separate contribution from the economist who is introduced after the completion of a plan: his rôle should be diffused, though his advice is admittedly often subordinate to political, social, technical and other elements.

Having helped to narrow the range of possible or suitable alternatives for, say, the long-term distribution of the population or the lay-out of an individual town, there may then be scope for detailed social cost-benefit analyses of the few alternatives finally selected.

Cost-benefit analysis
Cost-benefit calculations attempt to assess the total cost and benefit to society of individual investments, normally in an effort to judge among competing alternatives.[1] The idea of costs that are not borne by those responsible for them originated in the distinction drawn by the economist A. C. Pigou between private and social costs.[2] A favourite example of a social cost that would not be borne by the person or firm responsible for it is that of a factory with a smoky chimney. While the smoke is undoubtedly a cost to the community it is not one that is borne by the factory owner. A cost-benefit analysis of the possible construction of such a factory would include the cost or loss imposed upon society (i.e. the local community) from the factory smoke, though a cost-profit or

---

[1] The technique of cost-benefit analysis is further discussed in Chapter 3, pp. 48 and 50.
[2] *The Economics of Welfare*, Macmillan, 1926. For the background and present scope of cost-benefit analysis which can be understood by the non-specialist see G. H. Peters, *Cost-Benefit Analysis and Public Expenditure*, Eaton Paper 8, IEA, 1966.

commercial calculation would not do so.[1] If market prices are not being charged for goods or services, cost-benefit calculations aim to include both costs that would be borne by suppliers if there were a market for the product and those that would not.

The costs of investments are usually readily established and the major problems occur in identifying, measuring and valuing benefits to the community or the population concerned, eliminating double-counting for transfer payments. Incidentally, although often carried out by economists, it is not certain that cost-benefit analyses strictly belong to economics; their origin was in engineering,[2] and they assume that resources will be available to carry out 'desirable' investments.

An oft-quoted example is the 'economic' assessment of the M1[3] in which the increase in speed of the traffic expected to transfer to the motorway was estimated and the gains in vehicles' and drivers' time, savings in fuel, etc., were assessed. The major problem was in valuing savings in persons' non-working time and for this a wide range of values from 2s. to 10s. per person-hour had to be assumed,[4] with an almost corresponding effect on the estimated rate of return. The final rate of return was estimated to lie between 10 and 15 per cent in 1960, but the biggest difficulty was to interpret this rate of return and to decide whether the motorway was a worthwhile investment *as compared with the many alternative uses to which the resources could have been put.* Even later, the present author at least was unsure that a firm conclusion had been indicated.[5]

[1] Unless the state enforced clean air standards which prohibited smoky chimneys. The creation of smokeless zones is not costless and the consequence of such standards would be to transfer one cost of operation from the community to the factory owner, who would have to (say) pay higher prices for smokeless fuel or for installing a filtration plant.

[2] R. Turvey and A. R. Prest, 'A Survey of Cost-Benefit Analysis', *Economic Journal*, December 1965.

[3] T. M. Coburn, M. E. Beesley and D. J. Reynolds, *London-Birmingham Motorway - Traffic and Economics*, Road Research Technical Paper No. 46, 1960.

[4] It is crucially important in assessing the outcome of cost-benefit calculations to bear in mind the assumptions upon which they are based. In this case transport economists have by no means finally decided how to value leisure and travelling time. See for instance M. E. Beesley, 'The Value of Time Spent in Travelling: Some New Evidence', *Economica*, May 1965.

[5] D. J. Reynolds, 'The Economics of Rural Motorways', *Journal of Industrial Economics*, November 1961.

It is almost impossible to justify an investment by cost-benefit analysis because, for example, one would have to show that the resources allocated nationally to roads would yield a higher rate of return than if used on other things, that investment in London-Birmingham routes was the best road alternative open, and that the final form of the motorway was the best of a range of alternatives. For these reasons cost-benefit analysis is best at choosing between a limited range of alternatives and can only produce answers if based on many preliminary assumptions. But even then the results are open to interpretation or misinterpretation and are generally inferior to decisions based on the market, which should therefore be used wherever possible.[1] Indeed without a reasonably undistorted price system operating over much of the economy cost-benefit analysis is even more difficult, if not impossible.

Economics, money and prices

Finally, it is necessary to clarify the relationship between economics and money, finance and prices because there is a widespread misunderstanding that economics is solely concerned with money and that it exercises a dominant rôle in the subject. There is of course a complex inter-action between money and the regulation of the economy, but in the context of town planning it is more accurate to regard money merely as a measure of value which also facilitates the allocation of resources.

In the market sector of the economy rising prices (or, more accurately, rising profits) are an indicator to entrepreneurs that, relatively to consumers' demands, resources are in short supply in an industry. They will therefore be encouraged to expand output in that industry. The rise in prices assists in the efficient allocation of resources by attracting them to the points of highest profitability. Similarly where output in an industry is high relative to demand, prices and profits will fall and firms will tend to quit the industry in favour of more profitable industries elsewhere.[2]

Two qualifications are necessary. First, when prices are not charged to consumers for the purchase or use of goods or services (e.g. roads) or when they are fixed (e.g. many professional services)

---

[1] R. Turvey and A. R. Prest, op. cit.

[2] For a full discussion of the price mechanism see G. J. Stigler, *The Theory of Price*, Macmillan Co., New York, revised edition, 1952.

or subsidised (e.g. many agricultural products) the allocative function of the price mechanism does not fully operate. Secondly, unless there are competing suppliers selling broadly similar goods with free entry into the industry, so that producers are forced to compete with one another for the custom of consumers, the allocation of resources is not optimal and the industry is said to be operating under imperfect competition. But when these conditions are fulfilled the market or industry is known as perfectly competitive, and this ideal matches the goods produced to people's wants within the limits of resources, output and incomes.

It is thus important to break through the 'veil of money' to persons' wants and resources, which are the real issues that economics seeks to illuminate. For example, in discussing road pricing[1] we are not necessarily concerned with extracting more money from the road user or increasing his burden of taxation, but only with improving the productivity or efficiency of the transport system and town lay-out. Moreover, though the idea of road pricing was mainly academic in its origin, the practical or political difficulties provide no reason for refusing to analyse the device or to explore its possible advantages.

Though it would take us beyond the confines of this short introductory survey, it would be interesting to speculate how far planning controls on such matters as the location of industry, the siting of roads and other land uses would be necessary in an economy in which competitive markets existed for all goods and services.[2] Certainly many of the guiding and design functions of planning would remain but many other problems could be dramatically simplified. It is one of the main theses of this book that the use of road pricing, and the adoption of more rational pricing policies for transport, housing and other services such as connection to gas, water, electricity and telephone would take much of the strain off planning controls—and much of the arbitrariness out of them.

Conclusions

To sum up, economics is concerned with the objective expression of the subjective wants of individuals and the allocation of scarce

[1] See pp. 31—41 and Chapter 5.
[2] See pp. 2—3, 98—101, and 111 for a discussion of why intervention in the housing market is in practice necessary.

resources to meet them, using money mainly as a measuring-rod. Even where valuations are difficult or impossible, as with aesthetic aspirations and Professor Buchanan's 'environment', the economist is not hostile to their satisfaction nor *less* competent in assessing them than other professional people who may be less ready to admit their limitations. The economist schooled in the theory of alternative costs should, perhaps, understand better than most that prescriptions concerning the welfare of others are a difficult and dangerous undertaking in the absence of objective criteria for evaluating competing proposals. They should therefore be made with caution and humility.

Economics is most at home in the private sector of the economy where allocation is by price and less surely in the public sector, but this does not mean that economists are insensitive to other aspects. Although the economist's methods may differ from those of other professions with an interest in town planning, his broad ends, the creation of an efficient and satisfying environment but within the *inevitable* limits of our resources, seem nonetheless to be the same.

CHAPTER 2

DISTRIBUTION OF INDUSTRY, HOUSING
AND TRANSPORT

ALTHOUGH WE are in this book concerned primarily with urban problems—and we are now predominantly an urban people—it is nevertheless important to set town planning initially in a wider context, albeit somewhat briefly and inadequately. In this and the following chapter we shall therefore undertake a survey of some current developments and problems.

Initially consideration of general planning problems involves setting broad aims and gradually narrowing them so that they indicate policies and techniques and demonstrate the inevitable conflicts with which town planning is concerned.

Our over-riding aim is to maximise the welfare of our present and future populations, but this objective is much too wide and vague to be useful and must be made more specific. More concretely therefore we may postulate that people at present and in the future have and will have certain wants for goods and services including housing, transport, and amenities such as private and public space, rural surroundings and opportunities for social life and recreation. These wants may be satisfied within the limits of our resources by the production of goods and services, and by arranging a suitable physical lay-out and environment. Immediately this has been said, however, conflicts arise because the type and spatial distribution of industry and economic activity that might maximise output may make individuals' demands for space, transport and other amenities more difficult and costly to satisfy.

An appropriate definition of planning for this work then seems to be 'the attempt to maximise human welfare with special emphasis on the distribution of the population and the physical layout and environment'. This specification and its emphasis on human welfare is preferable to more common definitions of planning as a study of the best use of land, because they give an emphasis to land (and agriculture) which, except in the special conditions of the last two world wars, is not fully justified. The starting point in considering the economics of planning is meeting people's wants either through the market system or by the public sector (by legislation, executive action and control, taxation and subsidy).

It is obvious from what has been said that planning is potentially concerned with a very wide range of specialised but inter-related subjects—with location of industry, transport, housing, architecture and other amenities. But a comprehensive study of the contribution of all these matters would be impossible and indeed largely unnecessary because, although it must take account of influences from these sectors, planning is essentially concerned with deficiencies, with conflicts between private and social costs and benefits, with supplying (or protecting) commodities and services for which markets do not at present exist, or are inadequate, and with fitting the separate components of physical lay-out into a consistent and economical whole. Only these aspects of location of industry, transport, housing, etc., need therefore be considered in detail.

THE LOCATION OF INDUSTRY AND INDUSTRIAL TRENDS

In choosing an industrial location an enterprise often pursues many objectives but, to simplify, it may be assumed to choose the location that maximises profits or minimises the combined costs of transport, raw materials, production and distribution of its chosen output. The location of industry that results from the uncontrolled action of individual enterprises may not always be desirable on other grounds. In particular it may produce depopulation and under-utilisation of social capital on the one hand or 'excessive' congestion and concentration of the population on the other, with the associated difficulties of restricted access to the countryside, and heavy costs in accommodating motor traffic by urban road construction.

It is normally difficult to influence substantially and directly the distribution of industries such as agriculture and forestry with a widely spread factor of production-land. Similarly, industrial location must be close to the source of raw materials for extractive and other industries such as iron and steel where transport costs are relatively high in relation to total costs and the production process involves a substantial loss in bulk or weight. For a wide range of manufacturing industry, however, location may be altered relatively easily with no substantial and permanent effect on costs,[1] provided (and this is an important proviso) first, that expansions or other changes are large enough to produce self-supporting and potentially mobile units, and, second, that linkage with other firms and industries does not inhibit re-location.

Unlike agriculture, the extractive industries and manufacturing, service industries, such as retailing, wholesaling, entertainment, transport and construction, are normally dependent on local demands and cannot therefore be relied upon to sustain the prosperity of an area independently. The distinction between independent agriculture, extractive and manufacturing industries and dependent service industries can be drawn only roughly, for certain regions like London and the South-East 'specialise' in services and supply a national market in doing so. Thus it has been estimated that in 1951 half the service employment in Inner London[2] was serving a national market, the numbers so employed being equal to 5 per cent of the service employment in England and Wales. But recently employment in the service industries (widely defined as non-manufacturing and non-extractive industries and excluding agriculture[3]) in the London and South-Eastern Region in 1962 was 66.1 per cent of total employment as compared with 55.6 per cent for the United Kingdom.[4] Other areas of course, such as seaside resorts, specialise in the provision of services, but since they are widely scattered they do not have the locational significance of London and the South-East.

For the past 40 years at least unemployment has tended to be comparatively heavy in certain areas of Britain, in South Wales,

[1] W. F. Luttrell, *Factory Location and Industrial Movement*, National Institute of Economic and Social Research, London, 1962, Vol. I.

[2] City of London, Boroughs of Finsbury, Holborn, St. Pancras, St. Marylebone and Westminster.

[3] That is, construction, gas, electricity and water supply, transport and communication, distributive trades, insurance, banking and finance, professional and scientific services, miscellaneous services and public administration.

[4] M. F. W. Hemming, 'The Regional Problem', NIESR *Economic Review*, August 1963.

in the North-East, in Scotland and on Merseyside, and the proportions of the adult population working ('participation or activity rates') have been low. Hence the pursuit of full employment policy has encouraged not only the maintenance of a high general level of demand in Britain, but special measures to divert comparatively mobile industry to these areas of higher unemployment from areas of full or over-full employment. In recent years, location or distribution of industry policy has taken on increased significance with the emphasis of public policy on economic growth. The waste of resources represented by localised unemployment, the maintenance of a high general level of demand and employment (leading to inflation, wage drift and instability in the prosperous areas) and balance-of-payments problems[1] may endanger the whole process of growth (from which the resources for modernisation must come).

At first sight distribution of industry policy may appear to have little direct relevance to urban planning policy, for it is concerned primarily with the maintenance of full employment and diversification of industry and is administered separately from the planning system by an industrial Ministry, the Board of Trade. But more careful analysis reveals that the connection is close. Consider the question of why policy should be directed towards taking 'work to the workers' rather than 'workers to the work'.[2] In the immediate post-war period the short-term justification for a 'work to the workers' policy was that moving workers to work would waste social capital: housing, roads, sewage and other urban installations would need to be reproduced prematurely in the expanding areas.[3] This argument was always rather weak, since the standard of social capital in the depressed areas (development areas or districts as they have been called in the post-war period) was often low, and in the longer run would demand replacement in any case. Increasingly therefore the rationale behind distribution of industry policy has been the directing and steering of industry away from congested locations like London and the Midlands towards the development

[1] *Conditions Favourable to Faster Growth*, National Economic Development Council, HMSO, 1963.

[2] Or some intermediate policy, e.g. new industry in new locations towards which the unemployed or the population at large would be encouraged to migrate.

[3] H. W. Richardson and E. G. West, 'Must We Always Take Work to the Workers?', *Lloyds Bank Review*, January 1964.

areas. This reasoning is not immediately convincing: many of the development areas or districts are congested and it is not obvious why industrial development should be diverted from, say, an uncongested new town location in the South-East to a congested development district such as Merseyside.

The reason for discouraging industrial development in the more congested areas is not only the short-term additional costs of congestion on a road (or rail) system which must be regarded as relatively fixed in its terminal capacity in the short run. For in the longer run account must also be taken of the costs of re-arranging road systems, housing and other utilities to meet extra demands. Included in these costs will be the loss of rural amenities if more spacious accommodation of existing (or expanding) populations is demanded to meet technical progress (e.g. the motor-car) or higher living standards. This will result in urbanisation of the countryside and larger populations would need to travel further to reach the countryside, unless longer-distance dispersal were to be adopted (e.g. new towns).

An optimum policy for industrial development

Clearly the solution that distribution of industry policy is searching for, in common with the other aspects of planning, is *the point at which the economies of scale (or agglomeration) are equalled or exceeded by the diseconomies.* Industrial development and expansion, and the associated housing usually develop by comparatively small additions to existing factories and settlements which, being small in themselves, rarely provide the full range of social capital necessary to sustain the additions and thus impose extra strains on the existing urban fabric, particularly on roads and town centres. Up to the point at which the economies of scale equal the diseconomies (including loss of amenities) industrial development ought to be promoted, but beyond that discouragement is necessary.

Economies and diseconomies of scale are very difficult to define and even more difficult to quantify. They must therefore be considered somewhat pragmatically when questions of the 'ideal' distribution of the population are discussed.[1]

To grapple more closely with the problem of industrial location it is necessary to consider the machinery of control and the experience

[1] See Chapter 7.

under it since the war. Up to 1965, the control of industrial development has been carried out under the Town and Country Planning
Act 1947; it laid down that any new industrial building or extension
of 5,000 sq. ft. or over (with lower limits in certain areas as from
1965) required an industrial development certificate from the Board
of Trade certifying that the development was in accordance with
the 'proper distribution of industry' before planning permission
could be granted.[1] Under this regime industrial development was
restricted in areas of full or over-full employment, and permitted
(and encouraged by grant and subsidy) in development areas[2] of
comparatively heavy unemployment. Between 1945 and 1947,
when this policy was pursued with the most vigour, half the factory
space built in Britain was in the development areas. After 1947 the
proportion of factory space provided in the development areas fell
to a sixth.[3] Nonetheless it has been estimated that some 287,000
new jobs in the development areas were directly attributable to
government action between 1945 and 1962.[4] As from 1965 industrial
development has been regulated by the Control of Office and Industrial Development Act, which permits the lowering of the 5,000
sq. ft. limit in certain areas.

Industrial redeployment
During the post-war period changes have taken place in the national
industrial structure and employment which have had a significant
effect on urban and regional pressures. Changes in the national
industrial structure between 1952 and 1962 have been calculated
as shown in Table I.

The figures indicate that, with the exception of the engineering
and electrical industry, the biggest expansions in employment,
both in absolute and in relative terms, took place in the service
industries not in general subject to the industrial development

[1] Central Office of Information, *Town Planning in Britain*, HMSO, 1963.
[2] Reduced to districts with a high rate of unemployment (over 4.5 per cent
in 1960) by the Local Employment Act 1960, and subsequently termed
development districts. Thus certain parts of the older development areas
were excluded from preferential treatment, whilst other districts outside
the development areas were included.
[3] M. F. W. Hemming, *op. cit.*
[4] L. Needleman and B. Scott, 'Regional Problems and Location of
Industry in Britain', *Urban Studies*, November 1964.

TABLE I

Percentage Change in Main Industrial Groups, 1952 to 1962

Standard Industrial Classification	Change 1952–1962 %	No. of Employees June 1962 000's
Professional and scientific services	+43	2,203
Distributive trades	+34	2,975
Insurance, banking and finance	+32	589
Engineering and electrical*	+24	2,199
Other manufacturing*	+22	312
Paper, printing and publishing*	+20	632
Construction	+19	1,614
Miscellaneous services	+8	2,130
Vehicles*	+8	890
Metal manufacture*	+7	605
Chemicals*	+6	524
Gas, electricity and water	+4	397
Bricks, pottery, glass, cement, etc.*	+3	357
Metal goods (not elsewhere specified)*	+3	561
Food, drink and tobacco*	0	857
Timber, furniture, etc.*	−2	294
Public administration	−3	1,346
Transport and communications	−4	1,699
Clothing and footwear*	−7	595
Leather, leather goods and fur*	−10	64
Textiles*	−14	865
Shipbuilding and marine engineering*	−15	264
Mining and quarrying	−18	721
Agriculture, forestry and fishing	−25	592
All industries	+10	23,286

Source: M. F. W. Hemming, 'The Regional Problem', NIESR Economic Review, August 1963.

* Manufacturing industries as defined in the Standard Industrial Classification, 1958. Employment in these industries includes personnel of clerical or administrative status, so that service-type employment tends to be under-estimated by this classification.

certificate procedure and which could not easily be regulated by planning controls. They also show that employment in manufacturing industries increased by less than the national average, in

TABLE II

Explanation of Regional Increases in Employees, 1952 to 1962

Region	Actual increase %	Excess or deficit over UK average %	Explained by original composition %	Explained by growth %
Eastern and Southern	22·2	+12·7	+0·5	+12·2
South Western	20·0	+10·5	+0·2	+10·3
Midlands	13·1	+3·6	−1·1	+4·7
London and S. Eastern	9·6	+0·1	+4·3	−4·2
UK average	*9·5*	*0*	*0*	*0*
Yorks and Lincs	6·7	−2·8	−3·5	+0·7
Wales	6·4	−3·1	−3·4	+0·3
Northern	5·8	−3·7	−3·5	−0·2
Northern Ireland	4·3	−5·2	−5·0	−0·2
Scotland	3·9	−5·6	−1·3	−4·3
North Western	2·4	−7·1	−1·1	−6·0

Source: M. F. W. Hemming, *op. cit.*

service industries by more than the national average,[1] and that agriculture, mining and quarrying employment declined substantially, indicating some pressure towards increasing urbanisation.

In regional terms the calculations appear to show that the regions with a significantly larger share of the expanding industries than the national composition in 1962 were London and the South-East, and the Eastern and Southern Regions; those with a significantly smaller share of expanding industries (and thus with a larger share of the contracting industries) were the Midlands, Yorkshire and Lincolnshire, the Northern Region and Wales. If however we revert to the industrial structure of the regions in 1952 and consider how far the subsequent changes have been due to the original industrial composition of the region (assuming national rates of growth) and how far to larger or smaller rates of growth in the expanding industries in the various regions, a somewhat different picture emerges, as can be seen in Table II.

[1] More precisely employment in manufacturing industry increased by $6\frac{1}{2}$ per cent; in agriculture, etc., mining and quarrying decreased by 20 per cent and in the remaining service industries rose by 17 per cent between 1952 and 1962. It is possible that, in spite of rising output and population, employment in manufacturing industry will stop increasing within the next 20 years; in the USA, for example, employment in manufacturing has not regained its 1953 level. (*The National Plan*, Cmnd. 2764, HMSO, 1965.)

It can be seen from Table II that the expansions in the favoured regions and the contractions in the unfavoured regions were not the result of the original industrial structures of the regions, but largely of the growing industries expanding more in the favoured than the unfavoured regions and declining industries contracting more in the unfavoured regions and less in the favoured. Thus the regional effects of the changes in industrial structure in Table I were not attributable to the original structures of the regions and the inference commonly drawn from studies of different regional rates of growth—that they are largely due to changes in national industrial structure—is not true.[1]

Poor prospects for development areas
In spite of the effects of distribution of industry policy it is clear that industrial trends have intensified pressures towards urbanisation and increased pressures on the Eastern and Southern Region (i.e. on the expanding fringes of Greater London), the South-West and the Midlands, at the expense of the more northerly and westerly regions.

The faster growth of service industries as compared with manufacturing has special significance for distribution of industry policy, for industry is most likely to be mobile when employment is expanding, and service industries, being generally tied to locality, are not likely to be mobile. Even among the potentially most mobile service industries such as those serving national markets, experience in office dispersal has not yet suggested a high degree of mobility away from London.

It seems likely therefore that it will be difficult in the future to use distribution of industry policy and other controls on sources of employment to help disperse industry and population away from the congested, fast-growing areas. This weakness in current policy is especially serious because several, if not most, of the development areas are vulnerable in the long run; in particular the prospects for employment in coal-mining and ship-building in the old development areas (Scotland, the North-East and South Wales) must be regarded as doubtful in the future.[2] (See Table I.)

[1] M. F. W. Hemming, *op. cit.*
[2] *Central Scotland: A Programme for Development and Growth*, HMSO, 1963; *The North-East: A Programme for Development and Growth*, HMSO, 1963.

Inevitably post-war distribution of industry policy has had its limitations, the most important of which from the planning and economic points of view has been the emphasis on reducing localised unemployment by encouraging industry to move to areas with high unemployment or lack of industrial diversity. Often these development areas were badly located and inaccessible, lacking suitable industrial sites and with a low standard of social capital. A policy of selecting attractive intermediate locations as growth points would probably have been more successful. Such a move towards the selection of growth points within or near the problem areas of exceptional growth or decline is evident in the studies of Central Scotland,[1] the North-East,[1] and the South-East.[2]

HOUSING TRENDS

With rising population, increasing urbanisation and the demand for more spacious accommodation the pressure to expand housing on the outskirts of urban areas is considerable, although this process is to some extent contained by planning controls. The National Institute article[3] shows this pressure in terms of population in different parts of Britain. (See Table III.)

TABLE III
Exodus from Major Cities, 1951 to 1961

	Change in population 1951—1961	%
Lancashire		
Manchester	−42,041	−6·0
Liverpool	−43,348	−5·5
Other County Boroughs	−63,758	−4·0
Remainder	+162,940	+8·0
Warwickshire		
Birmingham	−7,034	−0·6
Remainder	+168,653	+22·5
London and South-Eastern Region		
Greater London Conurbation	−176,121	−2·1
Remainder	+363,064	+14·2

Source: M. F. W. Hemming, *op. cit.*

[1] *Central Scotland: A Programme for Development and Growth*, HMSO, 1963; *The North-East: A Programme for Development and Growth*, HMSO, 1963.

[2] Ministry of Housing and Local Government, *The South-East Study 1961–81*, HMSO, 1964.

[3] M. F. W. Hemming, *op. cit.*

TABLE IV

Changes in Employment and Population, 1951 to 1961

	Employment	Population
London Conurbation	+450,000	−200,000
Rest of Bedfordshire, Berkshire, Buckinghamshire, Essex, Hertfordshire, Kent and Surrey	+300,000	+960,000

Source: M. F. W. Hemming, op. cit.

The separation between home and work-place resulting from this peripheral housing development is illustrated by the case of the London conurbation in Table IV.

This peripheral growth of housing has three main effects:

(1) It increases travel distances to work. There is no objection to this consequence in principle, since it is a voluntary process,[1] *provided that travellers pay the full costs of their transport*, including the costs of the congestion they impose on other people. This question is considered in more detail under transport in this chapter.

(2) Although the immediate provision of social capital such as access roads or open spaces is usually adequate and often generous, it is a matter of general observation (since adequate data are not available) that both local shopping facilities and local sources of employment are frequently deficient. Dependent facilities such as shopping can be expanded if necessary and sources of employment are largely independent in any case: no major planning difficulty arises from these problems. But road transport facilities, as the Buchanan Report has shown, cannot be expanded easily. Development by accretion and dependence on existing facilities more or less fixed in supply normally results from the small scale of individual developments, few of which can warrant the provision of a full range of social facilities.

(3) Whilst access to the countryside by occupants of peripheral housing may be improved (depending on the occupants' original circumstances), peripheral housing developments reduce the access of existing inhabitants to the open countryside. The consequences

[1] Although insofar as people undertake long journeys to work in order to live in or near the open countryside, and the advantage is nullified by other similar developments, the process will be self-defeating.

of this process may be illustrated by a hypothetical example. Consider a circular city of one-mile radius with an original population of 100,000 evenly spread over the circle; it can be calculated that each person will travel on average a distance of 0.33 miles to reach the perimeter. Suppose that the population of the city increases by 10,000 to 110,000 at the same original density; the radius of the city will increase to 1.05 miles and the original 100,000 inhabitants will have to travel an extra 0.05 miles to reach the countryside, *an additional 15 per cent in average travel distance for a 10 per cent increase in population.* The additional 10,000 population must be housed somewhere and the gains to them must be balanced against the increased strain on urban facilities and, less important, the additional distances to be travelled to the countryside by the existing population.[1] The town planner must attempt such calculations for all feasible alternative locations.

Green belts and other planning controls

One of the ways in which the adverse effects of peripheral housing on access to the countryside may be averted is by the establishment of green belts (around major cities and conurbations) within which planning controls are more rigidly applied. The effect however is to encourage housing demand to jump the green belt[2] and to engulf the land allocations of neighbouring planning authorities for housing designed to cover normal (local) growth in population. Small-scale developers and would-be owner-occupiers can take these up, for planning permission is normally attached to development or use rather than to the owner or ultimate user. But for larger-scale local authority housing, substantial resistance and refusal may be experienced.[3] (See below under planning controls.) This process has the effect of mitigating some of the adverse consequences of peripheral housing development at the cost of longer travel distances and higher travel costs (unless sources of employment are also decentralised). But the problem has been exacerbated by low

---

[1] In the longer run some element of gain to the existing population may accrue from economies of scale, e.g. in a wider range of goods and services available, more frequent public transport, lower costs and prices, etc.

[2] D. R. Mandelker, *Green Belts and Urban Growth*, University of Wisconsin Press, 1962.

[3] *Ibid.*

rail season ticket fares which are particularly relevant in the conurbations where rail services are sufficiently frequent and fast to be
attractive *vis à vis* other forms of transport.

Although it is necessary to discuss the question of planning
controls in more detail later, it is nevertheless appropriate to consider
their broad effects on housing and housing policy, not least because
housing is the largest single user of urban land[1] (some 40 per cent of
the total in 1957) and planning controls probably bear most
heavily on it.[2]

Imperfection and control in the housing market

By restricting the transfer of undeveloped land to housing, planning
controls concentrate demand for housing, raise the price of permissible housing sites and encourage development at higher densities.
This tendency may be reinforced by insistence on high density as
a condition of planning permission and by subsidy for high dwellings. Thus a certain pattern of housing may be forced on the
community and this pattern may not be what the community would
prefer if given a free choice. Only if planning controls and subsidies
happen to have struck the correct balance between the social
costs and benefits will the result be optimal in the sense that it
efficiently allocates resources to consumers' demands.

Other imperfections[3] in the housing market which strengthen
powers to force a particular pattern of housing on the community
are the purchase and allocation of housing. In the private sector
restrictions on borrowing or on the proportion of present income
that will be accepted in repayment of loans exclude many households from buying modern houses, whilst in the public sector a
period of residence or marriage is an almost universal condition for

[1] P. A. Stone, *Housing, Town Development, Land, and Costs,* Estates Gazette,
London, 1963.

[2] According to Mandelker (*op. cit.*), analysing planning applications in
1958, 'Residential applications bulk large in the planning case load, and in
the administrative counties they form 40 per cent of the total. Most of
these applications are for single houses. The rate of refusal in these cases
in the administrative counties is higher at 13.4 per cent than the national
average for all cases'.

[3] I.e. deviations from the conditions that would be found in a competitive
market. See pp. 14—15.

obtaining a council house so that current demand is almost never fully met, particularly in areas of expanding employment and inward migration. Proportionately the resultant shortages may not be very large—even in the South-East Study[1] for example the 'shortage' in 1963 was estimated at 150,000 with 2½ million existing dwellings, a deficiency of 6 per cent. But housing is such a vital commodity that even a small relative shortage will make households accept what is available rather than what they would prefer. On the other hand the 'shortage' of housing[2] may be an important factor in deterring inward migration and maintaining equilibrium between expanding and contracting areas.

TRANSPORT AND ROAD PRICING

Are there any special influences on transport which necessitate or justify some intervention or indicate the appropriate lines of future policy? An obvious starting point is in the pricing of transport and of the different means of travel in particular. Broadly speaking the normal rules of pricing indicate that transport in general, and each means in particular, should pay their full costs including track costs, costs of congestion and accidents, although the 'social' consequences of withdrawal of services (both road and rail) may justify some special, temporary exceptions to this general rule.

A familiar and controversial subject[3] is the pricing of roads and railways. The road user does not pay directly for his use of track—the road—whereas the rail user is expected to contribute sufficiently to overhead costs to cover track costs. On the other hand the road user contributed, in vehicle licence duties, purchase tax on vehicles, and in fuel taxation some £900 million to general taxation in 1964-5,[4] whereas in 1964 the railways incurred a current deficit of £73 million (working expenses £541 million, gross receipts £468 million) which was increased to about £120 million by

---

[1] *The South-East Study 1961-81, op. cit.*

[2] H. W. Richardson and E. G. West, *op. cit.*

[3] British Railways Board, *Study of the True Relative Costs of Road and Rail Freight Transport Over Trunk Routes,* 1964; Transport Holding Company, *Road Revenues and Costs,* 1964.

[4] British Road Federation, *Basic Road Statistics,* 1965.

the inclusion of interest and other central charges.[1] It is hoped (somewhat optimistically) however that this deficit will be eliminated by the early 1970s through the re-shaping of the railways and by more efficiency, including the closure and contraction of unprofitable, lightly trafficked or duplicate lines and services.

The correct pricing of road and rail (not to mention individual classes of traffic and vehicles) is complex. The road problem is aggravated not only by the difficulties of estimating the costs of providing the road system but also by questions of taxation and revenue; if government is to raise a given level of revenue from taxation in the least harmful way, there is no reason in principle why any commodity or means of transport should not be taxed (assuming it is the least harmful way of raising revenue). Professor A. R. Prest[2] has attempted to analyse these questions and concluded that the costs of road maintenance and interest charges on the capital costs of re-producing the road system in 1962 would be some £470 million, and that road transport's due contribution to indirect taxation (assuming that all forms of expenditure were subject to the same rates of taxation) was some £185 million, giving a total of taxation required from the road user of £655 million—some £85 million less than the road user's contribution to general taxation in 1962. But since then the gap between road taxation and road expenditure has widened and probably cannot be justified in the narrow transport sense,[3] but irrespective of this, the taxation paid by road users in congested areas is of major importance for planning.

Road costs, congestion and pricing

There are several classes of traffic for which questions of costs and pricing are crucial. In roads there is the now familiar problem of traffic in congested areas. Some rationing of road space results from the variable part of road user taxation, the duty on road

[1] It may be noted that track costs in 1964 were some £91 million (British Railways Board, *Annual Report and Accounts*, HMSO, 1964), that is, even excluding track costs British Railways were scarcely 'paying their way' as a whole on current account.

[2] 'Some Aspects of Road Finance in the UK', *Manchester School*, September, 1963.

[3] G. J. Roth, *A Self-financing Road System*, Research Monograph 3, IEA, 1966.

vehicle fuels, currently 3s. 7d. per gallon. Taxation paid per vehicle-mile varies directly with fuel consumption, which is in turn related to the size and technical characteristics of vehicles. There is thus an incentive to economy in the use of fuel and, as a result, to the development of smaller cars. In practice taxation paid per vehicle-mile varies from about 1d. for a small private car to about 3d. for a medium-sized petrol-engined lorry under uncongested conditions;[1] rates are about 50 per cent higher under severely congested conditions such as occur in Central London and in the centres of other large cities.

The full costs (less taxation) of vehicle operation on existing roads include the costs of road maintenance, the value of resources used in the operation of the vehicle itself (less taxation), and the costs imposed on other vehicles by additional congestion. In order that the individual vehicle should cover its full costs on existing roads taxation per vehicle-mile should equal road maintenance costs plus costs imposed on other vehicles and users, 'marginal public cost' in the term used by the Panel on Road Pricing.[1]

Road maintenance costs are relatively low (less than ½d. per vehicle-mile in most instances) and 'marginal cost' only becomes significant under congested conditions when it is likely to be comparatively large. The report of the Road Pricing Panel estimated that for the average vehicle the costs imposed on other vehicles by the passage of one vehicle may approach 6s. per vehicle-mile at a speed of 8 m.p.h., about 3s. 6d. per vehicle-mile at a speed of 10 m.p.h., 1s. 1d. at 15 m.p.h., and about 4½d. at 20 m.p.h. For heavier vehicles, buses and lorries, these costs are likely to be up to three times as much. These estimates may be reduced if the evidence by Professor Michael Beesley[2] on the value of travellers' non-working time is accepted.

Thus there is a very large gap between the prices paid and the full costs of vehicle operation under congested conditions. To rectify this discrepancy a *lower* general level of taxation of vehicles (corresponding to real costs under uncongested conditions) has been widely suggested, to be supplemented by *charging for road use under congested conditions*, that is where journey speeds are below 15-20

[1] *Road Pricing: The Economic and Technical Possibilities*, HMSO, 1964.
[2] M. E. Beesley, 'The Value of Time Spent in Travelling: Some New Evidence', *Economica*, May 1965.

m.p.h. Such a system of road pricing has certain difficulties which will be dealt with more fully below (see Chapter 5), but assuming, as is likely, that traffic is responsive to charges, this system would have substantial consequences for urban planning.[1]

Rail—the subsidised commuter

Another lesser anomaly is the prevalence of low season ticket rates for rail commuters, although they are of major importance only in Greater London where British Rail accounts for some 35 per cent of commuters to the Central Area.

In 1964 the average season ticket fare was 1.42d. per passenger-mile but analysis of 2nd class 3-monthly season ticket rates to London in 1965 on the assumption of 540 journeys per year indicated a fare of about 2.2d. per passenger-mile for journeys of 10 miles, falling approximately linearly to only 1.0d. per passenger-mile for journeys of 60 miles, with an average fare of about 1.9d. per passenger-mile. A 500-seat passenger train, fully occupied for a full working shift, could be operated in 1961 for about ½d. per passenger-mile in direct costs and contributions to overheads.[2] But if equipment is installed to meet the commuting peak, which cannot be used outside peak hours or which can cover little more than fuel costs if it is used, such a train may only be fully utilised for a quarter of the period and the appropriate fare for peak operation at 1965 prices would be about 2.4d. per passenger-mile. If overhead costs were increased to cover current costs of replacing or expanding old depreciated assets such as terminal facilities, the relevant peak-hour fare would be higher still. The tendency to charge fares on the basis of past costs or book values of old assets rather than on current costs of replacement is also evident on London underground railways.

The deficiency of peak commuter fares as compared with the full long-run costs of operation may not now be very large—perhaps 25 per cent—and there would be difficulties in raising commuter fares substantially unless road pricing were adopted

[1] For fuller discussion of the economics of congestion see the Appendix to this chapter, pp. 37—41.

[2] D. M. Dear, 'Some Thoughts on the Comparative Costs of Road and Rail Transport', *Bulletin of the Oxford University Institute of Statistics*, February 1962.

simultaneously. Nevertheless there is little doubt in which direction policy should aim; it is absurd to charge less than full costs for travel in over-grown and over-congested areas. Because of commuters' heavy commitments to their present housing, any fare increases should be gradual to reduce hardship.

Town planning and rational transport pricing policies

If these deficiencies in pricing public services, and roads in particular, in congested urban areas could be rectified, transport and town planning problems would be simplified. First, if a congestion tax were applied to all vehicles, it would bear heavily on buses. But the occupancy of buses compared with cars[1] is so much higher that the impact per passenger-mile would be small and there would be a strong incentive to transfer from private to public passenger transport. Secondly, a congestion tax would generally raise the cost of travel in towns to the individual vehicle and hence reduce congestion. The final outcome in terms of centralising or de-centralising tendencies is rather difficult to determine. But, since a congestion tax will benefit public transport rather than private, insofar as travellers rely on public transport, the congested area will be made more attractive by the tax; insofar as they rely on private transport the area will be made less attractive. At present our cities, at least those with a population of more than about 100,000 (see Fig.3, page 85), rely predominantly on public transport, and the tentative conclusion of the Panel on Road Pricing[2] that our cities (in their present form) would be made more attractive by a congestion tax may well be true. In the longer term however, with much increased car ownership, a congestion tax (offset by general reductions in motor taxation) would in effect make the city less attractive to personal transport, rural or semi-rural areas more attractive, and would set up de-centralising tendencies for those activities which are dependent on attractive personal transport (e.g. shopping).

The effects of road pricing are likely to be harsher on road goods than on personal transport, because there is no ready space-saving substitute for urban goods transport whereas public transport is a close substitute for the private car. Pricing would thus tend to bear

[1] Buses have an average occupancy of about 20 as compared with 1.5—2.0 persons per car.

[2] *Road Pricing, op. cit.*

heavily on road goods transport and set up strong de-centralising tendencies on those activities which depend upon it such as industry, wholesaling, retailing and goods railheads. The strength of the de-centralising forces arising from road pricing will also depend on how strong an attractor the town or city was in relation to its competitors. A town which is very attractive and only contained by planning controls would suffer weak de-centralising tendencies from road pricing.

Much the same kind of de-centralising tendencies can be expected from the more realistic pricing of rail commuter services, even though the deficiency is less significant and the question is in practice only of importance in Greater London[1] and the South-East. Higher commuter fares would limit suburban and exurban spread, reduce housing and land prices at the perimeter, make the centres of the larger cities less attractive to actual or potential residents on the outskirts and thus encourage dispersal of economic activity.

On balance then it seems reasonably certain that the rectification of these deficiencies in transport pricing would set up de-centralising tendencies in the long run and to this extent stimulate a more even distribution of the population and of employment. Moreover, road pricing by rectifying deficiencies at their source may reduce reliance on long-term plans and controls and hence resolve many of the intellectual and practical difficulties in town planning.

No public assistance for the private motorist

It seems to be thought that road pricing would favour the rich at the expense of the poor. This is not strictly true. The aim of road pricing is to cut the *general* revenue from taxation of the motorist by, say, $£x$ and increase the revenue by specific taxation under congested conditions by $£x$: neither the poor nor the rich motorist would in general be worse off. In practice by more selective use of uncongested in preference to congested roads, motorists in general would be better off, although the rural or urban/rural motorist

---

[1] For this and for other reasons which are important in planning, dependence on public transport, dependence on rail for personal transport, dominance of Britain in locational terms, London is *sui generis* in planning terms, and many of the general arguments and conclusions of this work will not necessarily apply to London.

will tend to gain more than the purely urban motorist, who would probably have to pay more.[1]

The present 'free-for-all' on congested urban roads means that the private motorist, who is in general wealthier than the average, raises the costs of all other road transport: the resulting chaos imposes extra costs on people who are more often than not poorer than himself.

[1] Residents in highly priced, congested areas should receive special consideration.

APPENDIX

THE ECONOMICS OF URBAN CONGESTION

Road congestion

The economics of road congestion have been very fully covered[1] but the subject is so important that a brief simple survey is of some value in order to extract the implications for planning.

Let us assume that costs per vehicle-mile for all vehicles on a given road consist of a constant (a) plus an additional cost which increases in a straight line with traffic flow, equal to $\frac{bq}{W}$ where b expresses the effect of one vehicle per hour on average costs per vehicle-mile, q = traffic flow in vehicles per hour, W = road width in feet. Then the cost/traffic flow relationship is given by:

$$C = a + \frac{bq}{W}$$

and this is illustrated by the curve termed 'average cost' in the figure.

At a particular traffic flow,

then, say q_1, each vehicle bears a cost per vehicle-mile of $a + \frac{bq_1}{W}$. This does not give the total costs attributable to the passage of one vehicle, however, because each individual vehicle raises the costs of the $q_1 - I$ other vehicles by b. The total costs then attributable to the passage of one vehicle (the marginal cost) equals $a + \frac{2bq_1}{W}$ approximately and is given by the marginal cost curve in the figure.

Thus each individual vehicle *bears* a cost of $a + \frac{bq_1}{W}$ but *imposes* additional costs of $\frac{bq_1}{W}$ on other vehicles to give a total cost attributable to its passage of $a + \frac{2bq_1}{W}$. In other words, on the assumption that costs increase linearly with traffic, *each vehicle imposes as much congestion costs on other vehicles as it bears itself.*

To remedy this situation and

[1] *Road Pricing, op. cit.*

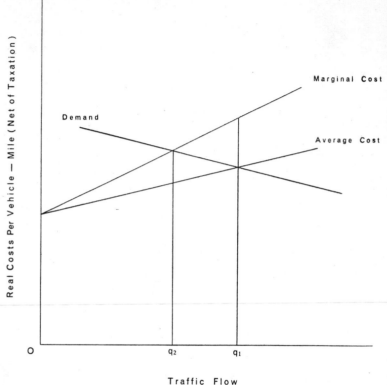

FIGURE 1. CONGESTION COSTS ON A GIVEN ROAD

to bring traffic flow into line with the full costs attributable to each vehicle trip, a specific charge, equal to the difference between average and marginal costs at the traffic flow willing to pay that charge, is commonly proposed. This charge will depend on road characteristics, demand and on the responsiveness of demand and must be found by trial and error.[1] It should be noted that the correct charge to secure economically efficient use of the road will exactly cover the cost of the road, if the road is the correct economic width for the traffic it carries, i.e. the traffic willing to pay the toll (given by q_2 in the figure). For the correct economic width will be that which minimises the total annual costs of the road plus the traffic it carries. In other words the aim is to minimise:

$$WRI + Hq_2 \left(a + \frac{bq_2}{W}\right)$$

where R=cost of widening road by 1 foot for 1 mile

I=rate of interest

H=no. of hours in year the traffic flow of q_2 is flowing.

This is minimised when:

$$W = \sqrt{\frac{bHq_2^2}{RI}} \quad \dots \dots \dots \text{(i).}$$

Now the correct charge per vehicle-mile will be $\frac{bq_2}{W}$ and the annual revenue from the charge, paid by Hq_2 vehicles, will be $\frac{bHq_2^2}{W}$. The annual cost of the road will be WRI and since $W^2RI = bHq_2^2$ (from (i) above) $WRI = \frac{bHq_2^2}{W}$; the annual cost of the road and the annual revenue from it are equal. This is a useful indication, in conjunction with other criteria, of whether roads are economically adequate or inadequate for their traffic. When the revenue from the charge is greater than the annual cost of the road the road is economically inadequate; when the revenue is less than the annual cost the road is economically more than adequate.

In practice in congested areas the simple straight line relationship between traffic and congestion does not hold and the curves slope upward at an increasing rate as illustrated in the report of the Panel on Road Pricing.[2] Thus the individual vehicle will impose more congestion costs on other vehicles than it bears itself, and the relationship between revenue and road costs will not hold

---

[1] Although using data representative of Central London (*Road Pricing, op. cit.*) it seems that the optimum charge under present conditions will approximate to 1s. per passenger car unit-mile for a wide range of elasticity (responsiveness) of demand which is probably the least known of the variables.

[2] *Road Pricing, op. cit.*, p. 46.

exactly. However the linear assumption is a useful approximation and simplification of the factors and relationships in urban congestion, and emphasises the value of a pricing system.

Other forms of urban congestion
Road congestion is merely one form of urban congestion, the phenomenon of 'getting in each other's way'. But there are others—queuing or walking on crowded pavements are two examples. We now explore other forms of urban congestion briefly to see whether the results of our analysis of road congestion shed any light on them and we ask whether people do tend to impose as much (or more) congestion on other people as they bear themselves.

To some extent it does seem to be so for other forms of urban congestion. For example, if in walking congestion takes the form of collisions, it is obvious that if one person collides with 10 other people, he has suffered 10 collisions and also imposed 10 collisions on *other* people. Again, to take a simple queuing problem, let us assume a shop with a permanent queue of 10 people each taking 1 minute to be served and, in equilibrium, with one arrival in the queue

every minute. The new arrival will endure 9 minutes' delay whilst the people ahead of him are served, but when his turn comes, his presence will impose 1 minute's delay on the 9 other people behind him. Again he has imposed as much delay on other people as he has borne himself. Further, in walking under congested conditions, even if no collisions occur, it seems that a similar phenomenon to road congestion takes place, in that an additional pedestrian will tend to slow down all other pedestrians and increase their 'costs'. This example suggests that urban pedestrians and queues should be taxed in the way suggested for road traffic, but provided that the price differentials between modes of transport (walking, public and private transport) properly reflect their different costs there is probably little further to be obtained by getting the absolute levels correct. It may be noted that commercial enterprises tend to reduce queues by supplying staff to meet demand semi-automatically.

It is difficult to see how far these kinds of relationships can be generalised, but over a considerable area of action and individual choice urban congestion seems to have the following elements: i) a noticeable cost or loss borne willingly (in a broad sense) by the individual and presumably taken full account of in his actions, choices and valuations;

ii) a similar or larger additional cost or loss imposed by the individual on other people, taking the form of a small cost or loss imposed on many other people who cannot usually be easily identified or compensated.

The significance of these two elements is that whilst the 'market' would take account of the former costs and losses, it does not take account of the latter. Broadly speaking it can be said that up to half the costs of congestion are currently accounted for by market forces; the other half (or more) can only be covered by planning policies, etc., or, preferably, by quasi-market measures such as road pricing.

CHAPTER 3

PLANNING CONTROLS, LAND VALUES AND GENERAL SURVEY

PLANNING CONTROLS UNDER THE 1947 ACT

IF IT IS difficult to rectify the current deficiencies in distribution of industry, housing and transport policy, we still have planning controls as the final regulator of development. The precise legal aspects and details of planning controls are extremely complex and it is possible to consider broadly only the aspects of importance for the economics of planning.

Currently town and country planning is regulated by the major Town and Country Planning Act of 1947, as subsequently amended by the Town and Country Planning Acts of 1954, 1959, and 1963 amongst others.[1]

The main objectives and provisions of the 1947 Act were to provide a 'desirable' pattern of land use by obliging local planning authorities (62 counties and 83 county boroughs in England and Wales) to draw up 20-year development plans (in map and written form to be revised every five years) for Ministerial approval. It further aimed to bring development (with exceptions such as agriculture and government departments) under control by making it subject to the permission of local planning authorities or a government department. Other aims and objectives were to facilitate the acquisition of land by public authorities and to deal with various questions of amenity, for example, preservation of buildings

[1] J. B. Cullingworth, *Town and Country Planning in England and Wales*, Allen and Unwin, 1964.

42

of architectural and historic interest. Development was defined as

'the carrying out of building, engineering, mining, or other operations, in, on, over or under land, or the making of any material change in . . . use'.

In deciding whether or not to grant planning permission the local authority was

'to have regard to the provisions of the development plan so far as material thereto and to any other material considerations'.

This procedure stands substantially unmodified.

The financial provisions of the 1947 Act, as modified by the 1954 and 1959 Acts, are of considerable economic importance. Under the 1947 provisions the state took over all development rights in land, and before any development could be carried out the right to develop had to be purchased by payment of a development charge equal to the difference between the existing use value of the land and its development value. Compensation for the loss of development values existing in 1947 was to be paid from a lump sum of £300 million reserved for this purpose and in these circumstances it was presumed that land would be bought and sold at existing use value, and that compensation for land compulsorily purchased by public authorities would also be at existing use value.

This system did not work satisfactorily.[1] The development charge was abolished in 1953 and a revised basis of compensation was laid down in the 1954 Act under which the owners of land who suffered loss of development value through planning restrictions were entitled to receive compensation up to the value of the established

[1] 'The imposition of a 100 per cent development charge in 1947 proved to be too onerous and the market threatened to break down . . . The development charge was not so much inhibitive of development as inhibitive on sellers, who now had no incentive whatever to part with their land when it was wanted by a builder. The developer paid the same amount for the land as before, but paid part of the price to the Central Land Board and part to the owner. The latter however received only the existing use value and consequently was unwilling to sell for this amount. The time it took for development charges to be assessed may also have had a discouraging effect. Moreover the development charge was determined largely on the basis of haggling between the owner and the Central Land Board and may well have fallen short of the true development value.' (H. Ronald Parker, 'The History of Compensation and Betterment since 1900', in Land Values, edited by Peter Hall, Sweet and Maxwell, 1965.)

claims on the £300 million fund. Owners of land compulsorily acquired by local authorities also received existing use value plus that of established claims.

The 1954 Act however set up a two-price system in land, full development value for sales in the private sector, existing use value plus value of established claims in compulsory acquisitions. The latter was generally lower. This dual system was changed by the 1959 Act, the effect of which was to compensate compulsory acquisitions of land at full market values, that is, the most profitable use for which planning permission could be deemed to be granted, with safeguards against payments for values created by the actions of public authorities (e.g. the acquisition of land for new towns).

Compensation for the refusal of planning permission
The question of compensation for refusal of planning permission is somewhat complicated and confusing. In general compensation for refusal of planning permission is either not made or only at the values obtaining in 1947; in practice few claims for compensation have been made under the 1954 Act. Where however refusal of planning permission is judged to have deprived the applicant of 'reasonably beneficial' use of the land in its existing use, compensation for loss of development value is payable at full market rates. This situation has been important in re-developing office space in central London, where old spacious properties with high rooms and wide corridors could be re-developed to the same *cubic* capacity (plus the 10 per cent allowed by the 1947 Act) with more floor space to accommodate larger numbers of workers.[1] Refusal of planning permission in these circumstances, which might have been justified to avoid strains on facilities resulting from further growth in central London, was prevented by the heavy burden of compensation payable, which may now rise as high as £10 per sq. ft. or £1,000 per employee.[2]

Both as a matter of equity and of ensuring the best use of land, market values are essential as the basis for public and private acquisition of land if the market (as modified by planning controls)

[1] This 'loop-hole' was closed by the 1963 Town and Country Planning Act which removed liability to pay compensation for any increase in *floor space* that was refused. (J. B. Cullingworth, *op. cit.*)
[2] *The Economist*, 7 November, 1964.

is to be the major allocator of land, and if the question of increments in land values can be solved satisfactorily (see pp. 51—2). The question of compensation for refusal of planning permission seems much more debatable. The deliberate extinction of an *existing* use in the public interest seems to merit compensation at full market rates, on the grounds both of equity and of the efficient use of resources. But *the extension* of an existing use which is clearly contrary to the 'general welfare' (i.e. total costs exceeding benefits) and which, but for compensation, could be expected to be refused planning permission, is much harder to accept. For offices this anomaly has been finally rectified by excluding compensation for refusal of office development permits, introduced in 1965.[1]

The machinery of development control

To deal with applications for planning permission the machinery of development control is applied. Outside county boroughs, which are themselves full planning authorities, the first stage in development control is application to the local district council, of which there are some 900. This stage of development control has been delegated to district councils by the county planning authorities.[2] If the application is approved by the district council it may be reviewed (and reversed) by the county authority, and if the result is refusal the applicant may appeal to the Minister. A public local inquiry is then held by an inspector on the staff of the Ministry, who may advise consent or rejection, but the final decision rests with the Minister who may reverse the recommendations of his inspector.

Several comments on this process are necessary from the viewpoint of economics and the 'general welfare'. First, for reasons connected with the difficulties and delays in making, reconciling, revising and approving plans, the development plan has not proved the clear guide and frame of reference for development control that was originally intended.

Secondly, although flexibility is essential in the administration of development control, and past cases cannot necessarily be taken

[1] Control of Office and Industrial Development Act, HMSO, December, 1964.

[2] D. R. Mandelker, *Green Belts and Urban Growth*, University of Wisconsin Press, 1962.

as precedents, the pattern of decisions has been criticised for inconsistency and failing to provide clear guidance on planning policy.[1]

Thirdly, although the procedure for appeal by the applicant on refusal of planning permission may be adequate, there is no corresponding machinery for appeal by persons who may be adversely affected by consents and who may in practice have difficulty in learning about planning proposals.[2]

Fourthly, delegation to local district councils (outside county boroughs), whilst giving an essential degree of local influence in planning decisions, means that an interested viewpoint may be taken, and it may be tactically difficult for the county planning authority or the Minister, who can be expected to take a wider view, to countermand earlier decisions. For this reason and also because of the undue burden of decision at a remote centre, regionalism in planning is often advocated, although the precise form this regional tier of government should take is controversial.

Fifthly, the burden of case-work is heavy and delay on controversial cases inevitable.[3] Some 462,000 planning applications were made in 1964; 18 per cent (83,000) were refused, and of these some 20 per cent (16,000) were appealed. With changes in planning and planning procedures however it is hoped to lessen this burden, and to rectify some of the other causes of criticism,[4] chiefly by attempting to separate broad 'strategic' planning from detailed plans.

Finally, although planning applications and demands for development are valuable indicators of demand—and they are essential if more extreme (and impossible) forms of *dirigisme* are to be avoided—the procedure of consents and refusals, even supplemented by discussions and modifications, may not by itself secure the best physical lay-out of a locality, a region or the nation. For the results of development control depend on the particular demands of the would-be developer, including the acquisition of a site from a willing seller, to be finally permitted, refused or modified in the interests of the 'general welfare', inasmuch as that elusive concept can be

[1] D. R. Mandelker, *op. cit.*
[2] J. B. Cullingworth, *op. cit.*
[3] D. R. Mandelker, *op. cit.*
[4] Ministry of Housing and Local Government, *The Future of Development Plans*, HMSO, 1965.

realistically interpreted. It is possible however that in some cases
the 'general interest' could be better served by the planning authority
taking the initiative, acquiring land in the optimum location
and directing demand towards it. This procedure is followed to
some extent by the provision of council housing and new towns,
although it is inhibited and distorted by conflicts between neighbouring planning authorities; also, although powers of land
acquisition by public authorities appear adequate, the procedures
are lengthy and difficult and there is a natural reluctance to use
them if demand can be met by the market.

Positive planning and the market for development

It seems however that in the conflict between pressure to expand
by peripheral development in the major urban areas and planning
controls, positive planning *could* play a part. The proposal to build
a new city of 250,000 in north Buckinghamshire, with tighter
control on peripheral urban development and reception of London
overspill population elsewhere in the county, is an interesting
example.

But the scope for positive planning is limited; powers of control
are essentially negative and developers cannot be forced to conform
to *positive* plans unless a pressing demand or 'shortage' exists.[1]

Similarly planning controls, which formally are strong, cannot
for ever be applied in the face of a strong market demand, particularly in the pressure for housing development on the outskirts of
growing urban areas. As indicated above, strong planning controls
in the face of a demand for development are likely to lead to a
substantial rise in land prices in that use, and it will be those prices
rather than the controls themselves which will choke off and regulate demand. Since land acquisition must be at market prices,
land values in general must tend to rise towards those attainable in
the most profitable use so that any long-run attempt to oppose the
market raises the cost of land acquisition by the local authority
itself. Sharp increases in land prices are especially probable when
known allocations of land are approaching exhaustion because
then the speculative element of demand will tend to take over and

[1] For this reason (apart from new towns where the planning authority
has almost complete ownership, control and initiative) some of the positive
and imaginative plans put forward, e.g. for nucleated cities, linear cities,
etc., are highly unrealistic.

withhold land from the market in order to take advantage of rapidly rising prices. Fortunately, perhaps, the strength with which planning controls may be administered in the face of a high level of demand and popular pressures is limited, at least where those pressures arise from within the planning authority's area.

How closely can development control reflect the myriad gains and losses which follow the granting or refusal of planning permission? Assuming that such gains and losses are quantifiable (which more often than not is untrue) they are of two kinds, large and accruing to a few individuals or small but widely diffused. The latter class are much harder to identify while those interests which make large gains or losses tend to be more vocal and highly organised. It is therefore an almost inevitable consequence of town and country planning procedures that sectional interests tend to be over-represented while the diffused voices of individual interests are not adequately heard.

The economics of development control
Under what circumstances should planning permission for particular developments be granted or withheld? With the exception of the work of Lichfield[1] much work remains to be done on this subject, and at best cost-benefit analysis can only be an imperfect indicator. The aim of planning is to guide development in directions that will maximise the sum of benefits to the whole community over total costs to the community (transfer benefits and costs being excluded) with the minimum aim that planning permission for a particular development should be refused if the total costs to the community are considered higher than the total benefits. Ideally refusals, discussions and consents should produce the pattern of development giving maximum net benefits.

Cost-benefit analysis then may be useful as an aid to judgement; it involves listing, quantifying and valuing the costs and benefits from the given development as far as possible, in order to gauge for example whether those other benefits that cannot be quantified justify the net remaining cost of the proposal. The heavy burden

[1] N. Lichfield, *Economics of Planned Development*, Estates Gazette, London, 1956, and 'Cost-Benefit Analysis in Plan Evaluation', *Town Planning Review*, July 1964.

of development control requires more rapid, if less sophisticated, methods of appraisal, however, and a possible alternative procedure is outlined below.

Since the market price of land and property in a particular use reflects its productivity in that use as measured by the market, the net profits obtained by the land owner or developer (or both) on the granting of planning permission and development can be assumed to reflect very roughly the market value of the net benefits to the community arising from that development.[1] Against this must be set the costs and benefits which are not currently valued by the market,[2] such as losses of 'amenity', costs of congestion or accidents likely to result from the proposed development.

Some examples may suffice to show how this technique may be used, and to illustrate the kinds of questions which must be asked and answered on development control.

(1)   Planning permission is requested for the construction of a house on a $\frac{1}{4}$-acre of agricultural land with a market value in that use of £50 and of £2,000 in housing use, the cost of roads, services, etc. being £500. The net profit or surplus is thus £1,450, and the question to be judged is whether the surplus is sufficient to compensate neighbours and passers-by for any net loss of visual amenity that may be suffered. Alternatively it may be asked whether the loss of visual amenity justifies a virtual 'tax' (imposed by planning control) of £1,450.

(2)   Planning permission is requested for an office development in the centre of a city, the estimated net profit from the development to landowner and developer being £1 million. The office expects to employ some 200 additional workers of whom 100 are expected to travel to work by car. Is the surplus of £1 million sufficient to compensate other people likely to suffer from the additional congestion on the roads (see Chapter 2), on existing parking space and on public transport resulting from the extra workers' travel? Alternatively, is the surplus of £1 million sufficient to cover the

---

[1] In practice the net profits attainable from development will only approximate to the net benefits to the community as valued by the market, because the land-owner or developer will rarely be able to set his prices in such a way as to extract all the net benefits for himself.

[2] Though some such costs could be valued by the market if proper pricing arrangements were made.

cost of road provision for the additional traffic (see Chapter 8), the net cost of providing for the extra parking and the net cost of expanding public transport?

Instead of application to develop in a specific use on one of several possible sites, a different problem is involved when several alternative applications or uses for a particular site—usually a key site in the town or city centre—are put forward. Here the objective must be to maximise the net benefits to the community from the site; this procedure would list, quantify and value the total costs and benefits for each alternative use of the site, with a presumption in favour of that use showing the maximum surplus of benefit over costs. (Shorter, less accurate approximations may be used and the results compared.) Thus the office example in (2) above may be compared with the use of the site as an open space. Then the question is whether the surplus of £1 million is sufficient to cover not only the additional costs of congestion attributable to the office but also the estimated benefits from the use of the site as open space.

There are obvious difficulties in quantifying and valuing the benefits of open space and also in applying cost-benefit techniques to planning and trying to 'measure the immeasurable'. But if planning controls are to be strongly applied it is necessary to reduce even imperfectly the capricious and arbitrary elements in planning and the administration of controls. And even though cost-benefit analyses cannot give the full or certain costs and benefits of any development they can to a certain extent narrow the range of indeterminacy in knowledge and decision-making.[1]

There can be substantial differences between cost-benefit analyses and 'financial' assessments. Cost-benefit analyses attempt to identify the value of real resources used in development and to compare them with the estimated value of real net benefits *from the viewpoint of the whole community*. Financial, commercial or cost-profit assessments tend however to be made from the narrower point of view of the private developer or local authority, and may include subsidies as an offset to costs, additional rate revenue and other transfer payments which are neither costs nor benefits to the whole community in a real sense. The connection between economics and finance in this context can be complex, with many pit-falls, but

[1] For further discussions of cost-benefit analysis see references in footnotes to pp. 13—14.

broadly speaking the ideal is to make as wide an assessment as possible while trying to ensure by planning and other policies that financial incentives will conform.

LAND VALUES

Land values are of some importance, partly because of the familiar question of taxation of increments in land values (which in practice has little direct relevance to planning) but mainly because land as a factor of production in economics has certain peculiarities.

Initially land can be regarded, like air, as being supplied free by nature in fixed inexpansible quantities, so that it will acquire a price or value according to the supply and demand for its attributes (fertility, climate, minerals, position, etc.) According to these attributes land will develop a price corresponding to its most profitable use, if allocation is by price within a free competitive market.

Consider however a town where land is not allocated in a free market and in which demand for housing land on the perimeter is high but around which the supply of land for housing is restricted by planning controls to exactly the desirable extent, whatever that may be. In this situation agricultural land for housing at the perimeter with a typical capital value of £200 an acre, corresponding to its productivity in agriculture, may be worth £10,000 an acre if developed for housing at, say, 10 houses to the acre.

Assuming that the provision of roads, services, etc., will cost £500 a site, a total of £5,000 per acre, the land-owner will be left with a windfall gain of up to £4,800 an acre arising from planning controls and the granting of planning permission for his site. Without these controls he would presumably be willing to sell at something more than £200 an acre which would then be the market price for undeveloped agricultural land supplied for housing. If planning controls and planning policy in general have struck the correct balance, it may be desirable that high prices for housing land should continue in order to give the correct incentives towards efficient land utilisation. But there is a case in equity for trying to tax away these wind-fall gains to land-owners.

The development charge and alternatives

The difficulty, of course, is to avoid restricting the supply of land to the market from less valuable to more valuable uses and thus raising land prices.[1] Two factors are important, the nature of the development charge (its size, permanence, method of payment) and the elasticity of supply of land, that is, how readily it will be supplied from a less valuable to a more valuable use. Many proposals on development charges have been made in recent years; the most promising seems to have been that suggested by Professor A. C. L. Day[2] who has argued for a charge of less than the full increment in land values (e.g. 50 or 75 per cent) to be made as a condition of planning permission, which would in effect simply be *sold* for a given charge. The size of the charge could perhaps be varied (within limits) according to the desirability of the proposed development in planning terms. In the event the government proposal[3] is for a levy of 40 per cent rising to 50 per cent, to give an incentive to owners to offer their land for development.

Concerning the supply of land for development, with a large differential between existing use value and development value such as is likely to exist for virgin land, a development charge of 40 to 50 per cent (rising with time) may not reduce the supply of land for development so long as it is believed to be permanent. For the re-development of existing sites, however, the effect of a development charge is likely to be restrictive. If the administrative problems of imposing a development charge can be overcome, insofar as it is planned to take place on land already developed its effects will be strong therefore.

As a more equitable alternative to the development charge, and to make the granting of planning permission less arbitrary, there are attractions in the idea of obliging developers to obtain or purchase the consent of persons affected as a condition of planning permission. The problem of obtaining the consent of all people adversely affected is a major difficulty in planning, whether for public or private development. To require the consent of all persons affected would be virtually impossible and lead to almost complete *immobilisme* on development. Yet some weight

[1] D. R. Denman, *Land in the Market*, Hobart Paper 30, IEA, 1964.

[2] A. C. L. Day, 'The Land Boom and the Community', *Westminster Bank Review*, May 1964.

[3] Ministry of Land and Natural Resources, *The Land Commission*, Cmnd. 2771, HMSO, 1965.

should be attached to their interests and present planning procedures are hardly satisfactory. By defining the limits within which compensation and consent are required a practical scheme might be devised to cover some cases and this approach appears the most fruitful for the future development of planning policy.

How are land values determined?

An important question is how land values arise, particularly those in urban areas which (modified by planning controls) are mainly determined by position in relation to the main point or points of attraction.

In general, values for developed land will be determined by transport costs to the particular point (or points) of attraction that has (or have) stimulated development, though this statement is an over-simplification. Thus consider a development, such as housing, in a straight line in a standard type of house built on plots of standard size arising only from a single point of attraction, say a factory, at a point P (Fig. 2). Then if development is no longer worthwhile and attractive beyond point Q, and each head of household travels to the factory once per day, transport costs per period (say per annum) may be represented by curve PT, diminishing to zero as the factory is approached. With competition between dwellers, however, and assuming the factory is not repulsive, it is obvious that houses near the factory will command a premium inversely related to personal transport costs. Since this premium arises from

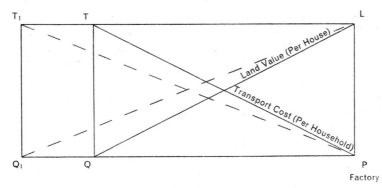

FIGURE 2 TRANSPORT COSTS PER HOUSEHOLD
AND LAND VALUES
(in current terms)

position it will finally adhere to the land, and if the land has no value in any other use, the curve of site and land values will be QL, rising as the factory is approached.

To generalise this simplified relationship is difficult and dangerous, but broadly speaking the individual demand for development or the occupation of existing premises will tend to settle on the location or premises which minimises the costs of meeting the individual user's wants and his desired pattern of travel to meet his other wants. Competition between users will then ensure that land values are high near points of general attraction and accessibility to many people, such as town centres, and diminish with distance from them. For example, if the factory in Fig. 2 is the only point of attraction in a settlement, land values will tend to diminish in proportion to increasing distance from it.

The tendency for site prices to diminish with distance from the main centres of London and Birmingham is shown by the work of Dr P. A. Stone[1] on prices of housing sites, but since sites tend to become larger with distance, prices *per acre* fall more rapidly, and in practice of course land values within an urban area will vary sharply and bewilderingly depending on actual, possible and permissible use, position and tenure.

Another urban land values problem is how far, and in what circumstances, should they be treated as a valid cost of development? For a given land use on a particular piece of land, the value will reflect the productivity of the land in that use, so that if a single development and a change in use is contemplated (other things being equal) the market value of land in its existing use is a valid cost of development. In effect the new development must bid away the land from its existing use by being more productive so that the developer can offer a price higher than the land can command in its existing use, although planning controls will tend to raise market values above opportunity costs, i.e. the value of alternatives foregone.

In another sense, however, in terms of the burden of development on the scarce resources of the whole economy, it seems that land

---

[1] P. A. Stone, 'The Prices of Building Sites in Britain', in *Land Values*, Sweet and Maxwell, 1965.

values cannot be regarded as a cost. Dr Stone[1] puts the matter thus:

'The community possesses a set of sites, no resources are used in the mere transfer of the sites from one group of users to another. Therefore providing that the resources used in the development of sites and in the adjustments made as a consequence of the transfer of sites are counted as costs, it is unnecessary and indeed incorrect to include in the costs the prices at which the sites were transferred.'

The Report of the Steering Committee on *Traffic in Towns*[2] has made the same point on urban renewal; land acquisition will impose no strain on the resources of the economy as a whole, although for *sections* of the community, such as road and planning authorities or developers, land values and costs may be a considerable burden or asset.

Planning and the regulation of land values

Another significant question is how far land values are important as an objective in planning; for example, how far should planning aim to maximise, minimise or maintain land values? In general, as shown in Fig. 2, since land values are merely a reflection of points of attraction, position and transport costs, they can have no independent validity as a planning objective. Planning should merely aim at the optimum layout by comparing the advantages and costs of various developments and the effects on urban land values would be ignored as a planning objective or effect.

For example, urban land values arise from the concentration of land uses, and if the optimum layout for a particular town or city were towards greater dispersal, particularly of central uses and developments, the effect of planning policy would be to reduce urban land values.

It is true that in a free market for land the rise or fall in land values might reflect certain changes fairly closely. Thus in the example in Fig. 2, if transport costs to the factory fell to PT_1, land values would tend to rise correspondingly to Q_1L. But such are the dangers of double-counting (particularly of adding increments in land values to reductions in transport costs to which they are attributable), the

[1] P. A. Stone, *Housing, Town Development, Land and Costs*, Estates Gazette, 1963.

[2] G. Crowther (Chairman), *Traffic in Towns*, Report of Steering Committee, HMSO, 1963.

distortions that might result from planning controls, and the difficulties in measuring overall losses and gains in land values, that more direct estimates of planning effects must normally be preferable.

Thus whether urban land values are, or are not, a cost to the community seems to depend on the viewpoint adopted; from that of the individual developer or authority they are a cost that must be borne, but from the viewpoint of the whole economy they are a transfer payment.[1] For these reasons it is important to separate land and property acquisition costs from construction costs in economic and planning assessments. And since urban land values are merely reflections of other factors there is little merit in making the regulation of them a primary independent objective of town and land-use planning policy.

Agriculture and rural land: a special problem?
Should preferential treatment be given to agriculture in planning and general economic policy? The 1947 Town and Country Planning Act and subsequent Acts have in general exempted agriculture from planning controls and included the protection of agriculture and agricultural land against development as one of the main aims of town and country planning. The Agriculture Act 1947 and subsequent acts[2] continued subsidies in the form of guaranteed prices and deficiency payments, supplemented by grants towards expenditure aimed to increase productivity, originally in the interests of home food production and later (when the importance given to home food production declined) in order to increase productivity and to maintain farm income.

Thus both through financial aid and in its special position in planning, agriculture enjoys protection and this dual protection has raised some important issues. Presumably agricultural support can be expected to reflect the importance of home food production in the balance of payments, or any other special virtues attributed to agriculture. These virtues in turn should then be expected to be reflected in the price of agricultural land, which, by making farming

---

[1] A transfer payment is made from one person to another or from the state to an individual other than for a productive service, and therefore redistributes national income and wealth without increasing it.

[2] G. Houston, 'The Control of Subsidy Expenditure: Agriculture', *Scottish Journal of Political Economy*, February, 1963.

TABLE V
Estimated average prices per acre for residential building land, 1960 to 1962

Region	Distance from the centre (miles)	Density (dwellings per acre)					
		5	10	15	20	30	40
				£000's			
London	5	12	17	23	28	39	50
	10	10	14	19	23	32	41
	20	7	10	13	16	22	28
	40	3	4	6	7	10	13
	60	1	2	3	3	5	6
Birmingham	5	8	11	14	13	27	
	10	6	8	11	13	18	
	20	3	5	6	8	10	

Source: P. A. Stone, quoted in D. R. Denman, *Land in the Market,* Hobart Paper 30, IEA, 1964.

more attractive, must be raised by agricultural support. But even in this favoured position the average price of agricultural land was only some £200 per acre in 1964 as compared with the figures given in Table V for developed land.

This argument indicates that further protection of agricultural land by planning controls is superfluous, and protection is the conventional way in which rural amenities, presumably to be enjoyed mainly by the town-dweller, are supposedly safeguarded. But the interests of agriculture, as interpreted by the application of planning controls, may by no means coincide with those of the town-dweller in his demand for rural amenities. Indeed they may be sharply opposed, for crops and farm animals normally require enclosure whereas the town-dweller may demand access.

It is unsatisfactory to rest one set of objectives on another in the hope that they will coincide, and this approach has probably inhibited the application of more positive policies to the question of rural land use. Little effort has been made to find out what people really demand of the countryside and attempt to give it to them. It seems paradoxical to protect the countryside so strongly in the legislation and administration of planning, with no clear idea of the purpose behind protection. Green belts are a similar example of almost instinctive intervention. While they have as their purpose a mixture of laudable objectives such as limitation of conurbation size and congestion and the preservation of rural amenities, one may be forgiven for wondering whether their chief result has not been the perpetuation of the cabbage!

Another general view which has been influential is that because Britain is already densely populated and its population is expected to increase substantially by the end of the century, and because land is scarce and in fixed supply, we should restrict the geographical spread of towns while promoting higher population densities within them than have been conventional in recent years. This view may be true but it is by no means certain.

In the first place, though land itself cannot be imported, many of its products can. If they sell competitively in Britain, our 'shortage' of land is thereby relieved, a fact of some significance for future agricultural policy.

In the second place, recent estimates brought up to date indicate that 80 per cent of our population living in urban areas occupy only 10.8 per cent of the land area[1] of England and Wales and it is not obvious why an urban 90 or (say) 95 per cent of our population occupying (say) 20 per cent of our land area should be an unsatisfactory distribution.[2]

The attitude that Britain is or is likely to be over-crowded seems the result of a kind of optical illusion, arising from the fact that most people live in large expanding cities, tend to visit attractive and crowded places at the coast or in the country, and rarely visit unattractive undeveloped countryside for obvious reasons. Thus they are not aware of the availability of open space and tend to ignore it.

Rural land near London and the other conurbations is of course very scarce (hence the attitude of their inhabitants to rural land), but with careful dispersal and a more even distribution of urban population it would be possible to develop at lower densities with little effect on the total amount of rural land and access to it. A policy of dispersal would encounter difficulties which must be considered

[1] R. Best, 'Urban Land Requirements', *Town and Country Planning*, 8 September, 1964.
[2] Thus Best estimates that by the year 2000 the maximum figure for urban land in England and Wales would be 7 million acres or 19 per cent of the total.

in more detail later (see Chapter 7), but the argument that Britain is over-crowded and *therefore* that we should live at higher densities is not the self-evident truth it is sometimes held to be.

A FUNDAMENTAL DECISION

An over-riding problem common to all the questions dealt with in the first two chapters—the distribution of industry and regional development, housing, transport, and planning controls—is how far we should retain our towns and cities in their present form, some with expansionary pressures to be regulated (probably with limited success and some hardship) by pricing or planning controls, others with a tendency to decline, partly because of their poor physical state and lack of attraction for growing economic activities. How far should we encourage and plan for dispersal to new or expanded towns which could relieve expansionary pressures in the larger cities and offer more attractive alternatives?

As will be seen later this choice confronts us both when we consider the Buchanan Report on the accommodation of traffic in towns and also in our discussion of urban renewal. Since it is the major decision to be taken in planning it will be examined more thoroughly in Chapters 6 and 7.

CHAPTER 4

TRAFFIC IN TOWNS:
THE BUCHANAN THESIS AND ITS APPRAISAL

The thesis

IT IS useful to consider briefly the background to the Buchanan Report[1] before appraising its approach.[2] After the war rising traffic volumes (which reached the pre-war level in 1950 and doubled again by 1960) led to pressure to expand the road system, and both for rural and urban roads alike the accepted remedy for traffic growth and increasing congestion was simply to expand the road system.

During the 1950s however it was gradually realised that the urban traffic problem was much more complex than this simple view, and a body of opinion (economists, architects, planners) grew up favouring as a solution either restriction, to protect the 'environment', or pricing, for example by charging each vehicle the costs of congestion imposed on others. In the late 1950s the conflicts between the 'expansionist' and the 'restrictionist' approach were clearly holding up both planning and transport solutions to urban problems[3] and Professor Colin Buchanan was appointed in 1961 to consider the problem urgently. His final report appeared in November 1963. For such a massive and apparently intractable problem, the timing of the Report was significant, especially as it was undertaken with a strong planning viewpoint but with little previous background of planning research or contact between planning and transport. The economic content was small. In this situation the Report is best regarded as an attempt to reconcile

---

[1] D. J. Reynolds, 'Congestion', *Journal of Industrial Economics*, April 1963.
[2] *Traffic in Towns*, HMSO, 1963.
[3] D. J. Reynolds, *op. cit.*

the expansionist/restrictionist conflict, to consider the problems of accommodating future urban traffic volumes, and as a stimulus to more systematic and realistic study of urban traffic and planning questions.

Briefly the Buchanan thesis or synthesis—for it is probably in the synthesis of several different approaches that Buchanan's main contribution lies—can be stated as follows. The rapid increase in vehicle ownership in Britain could be expected to continue, particularly in cars, which were unlikely to be superseded by other transport forms, and the ownership of which was likely to reach a saturation level equal to the present rate of vehicle ownership in the USA of about 400 vehicles per 1,000 population by about the end of the century. It seemed reasonable to suppose that our towns and cities could and should[1] continue to exist broadly in their present form, so that the growth of vehicle ownership and increasing population would impose severe, indeed impossible, strains on existing urban road systems and urban environments. To meet these strains it was necessary to carry out land use/transport surveys to forecast *future* traffic demands in order to establish road networks to accommodate traffic and segregate it in order to protect the 'environment'. Finally areas should be established in which traffic would be subordinate to 'environment', to pedestrians, quietness, safety, absence from fumes, and so on.

A large amount of road construction and other adjustments would be required which would be aided by the demands and opportunities for urban renewal over the long planning period suggested, 40 years. Above a certain size it would be physically or economically impossible to accommodate all traffic wishing to enter our towns and cities, particularly so-called 'optional' traffic (see Chapter 5).

> 'There are absolute limits to the amount of traffic that can be accepted in towns, depending upon their size and density, but up to these limits, provided a civilised environment is to be retained or created, *the level of vehicular accessibility a town can have depends on its readiness to accept and pay for the physical changes required. The choice is society's.*' (para. 444)

[1] Thus para. 60: 'although persuasive arguments can be adduced in favour of urban dispersal, this island is not big enough for large-scale dispersal if a sensible relationship is to be maintained between developed areas and open country.'

APPRAISAL

In recognising the substantial step forward taken by Buchanan in high-lighting the urban traffic problem (particularly in the short time available to him and his team), it is nonetheless necessary to question whether the thesis is either consistent or realistic. The subject is so vital that all doubts must be raised and resolved if possible, the more so since some of them are on important issues and problems

The self-defeating assumption

In the first place although the chain of reasoning from start (towns and cities broadly in their present form) to finish (restrictions on traffic) may be satisfactory, can rigorous restriction of traffic ever achieve equilibrium? If not, will the end product be consistent with Buchanan's original starting point? Here of course the problem is that with almost universal car ownership[1] restrictions on car use in large towns and cities will encourage patterns of travel and development away from the restricted areas. The trend may be towards the dispersal of activities within existing boundaries of development, particularly around town centres where future opportunities for urban renewal may be useful, or in completely fresh development in the countryside. In either case however restrictions on traffic will tend to direct development elsewhere so that the eventual equilibrium seems likely to be dispersal of development with no restrictions on traffic. Development controls could restrain this trend to some extent, but there seems no reason why a policy of short-term restriction of traffic, long-term accommodation, accompanied by planned dispersal, should be unsatisfactory.

Some idea of the process by which equilibrium between traffic and central lay-out—the critical relationship—may be achieved, can be gained from applying the theoretical work of Dr R. J. Smeed on town traffic.[2] With certain basic assumptions, in particular that the *ground space* required per worker is 100 sq.ft., Dr Smeed has calculated the size of the central area required and the proportions devoted to roads, parking and working space for different numbers of workers and for different means of transport. Assuming

[1] Buchanan assumes about 1.3 cars per family in the year 2010.

[2] R. J. Smeed, 'The Traffic Problems in Towns,' *Manchester Statistical Society*, 8 February, 1961.

a city of 200,000 population and with a working population of 100,000 (all working in the centre) Dr Smeed's methods can be used to show that for bus transport on narrow roads the total central area required will be 0.385 sq.miles. Of this 4 per cent or 0.015 sq. miles would be required for roads and none for parking. A universal transfer from bus to car (at current occupancies of 20 and 1.5 persons respectively) operating on urban motorways with multi-level parking, would require an increase in the total central area to 0.43 sq. miles. Of this 6 per cent would be required for roads and 11 per cent for parking, a total of 0.073 sq. miles. In other words the ground area devoted to transport would need to increase by about five times, and even this would not measure the full burden of the change because a large proportion of the whole of the town centre would need to be laid out afresh.

If however central employment was decentralised at the same time as the transfer to car transport took place, a different equilibrium would result. If the number of central workers were reduced to 50,000 and car transport was universally used, the size of central area required would be 0.21 sq.miles of which road would take up 4 per cent (0.008 sq.miles) and parking 11 per cent (0.023 sq.miles), a total of 0.031 sq.miles. In other words a halving of central working population would yield more than enough space to accommodate a transition from bus to car as the universal means of transport. Total central area space and total road space would be more than adequate, despite the fact that the need to provide parking would double the area devoted to transport. Even with the decentralised solution, of course, fundamental reconstruction and a new lay-out for the town centre would probably be required, *but the physical difficulties in accommodating the ultimate level of traffic, emphasised by Buchanan, would not occur*; in particular the problem of intersections and their frequency on the required road network (apparently *the* critical factor) would be much eased by decentralisation.

The point on cities remaining in their present form *versus* dispersal may be made in a somewhat different way. From the long-term approach of the Report and its reliance on urban renewal as an opportunity for reconstruction, it is clear that Buchanan was relying quite heavily on depreciation, obsolescence and massive investment to provide the substantial opportunities for fundamental re-development that his programme would inevitably entail. But given such opportunities for change, why should we keep our towns and cities 'broadly in their present form'? The Buchanan proposals thus undermine the basis of his initial assumptions.

Problems of collective choice

In the second place, there is the Report's conception of choice quoted above (page 61). This simple statement conceals enormous questions and raises, rather than resolves, intellectual, economic and political problems which are fundamental to the whole matter. The report stresses that there must be some balance between car ownership and road provision. The point is of course that whilst the price mechanism provides a well organised and developed system of supply to meet the demand for vehicles there is no such simple straightforward mechanism of choice in the case of roads. Analysing the question a little further an initial reason why this simple mechanism does not and cannot exist is that the road user does not demand roads as such at all. He does not and cannot say 'I want to buy this car and to pay for an extra yard of road to be added to the nation's road system'. His demand is for the use of existing road facilities and depends critically on his timing, mode and direction of travel. His effective demand can only be inferred from his use of the road and the amount he is prepared to pay for it.

In rural road provision the problem is comparatively simple because in general the road user pays in taxation sufficient to cover the cost of road provision and the costs of congestion he imposes on others; few alternative routes are available so that by measuring traffic flows and supplying road space according to conventional standards the solution can be clear and straightforward. On the other hand in large towns or city areas the road user (in particular the car driver) does *not* pay the full cost of congestion he imposes on others so that road use is not regulated by charging full costs and *no adequate investment criteria therefore exist.* The situation is further complicated by the critical effect on traffic volumes, and thus on the apparent 'need' for road investment, of the choice between public and private transport, and by many close alternative routes and policies. It is true that if a sufficiently sensitive system of road pricing could be evolved and applied, the resultant revenues would be a good indication of total effective demand for urban road investment, but which roads to build or improve would still remain a problem, though a much simpler one.[1] In urban areas there will always be a range of alternative solutions to a particular problem; narrowing the range of choice and securing consistency between solutions to different problems can be a considerable task.

Having briefly covered the problems of economic choice we can move on to the problem of political choice; for Buchanan's phrase 'The choice is society's' implies some collective political decision over and above choice *via* the price system. What chance is there that the ballot box and other democratic processes will give us rational choices in this matter? Electorates (national or local) cannot of course choose the most desirable alternative in a complex matter such as town planning, even if all the alternatives could be presented to them. They can merely choose between candidates and parties in all their aspects and policies, of which town planning will be only one, if it is an issue at all. Inasmuch as a solution *via* the price mechanism—which Lord Robbins has likened to a continuous referendum in the market with consumers 'voting' their preferences with their money (demands)—is bypassed or technically impossible, choices must be made at a more restricted technical or political level and accepted, rejected or tolerated by the electorate. As Professor W. J. M. Mackenzie[2] has pointed out in his analysis of Buchanan, there are at least four separate sets of interest and conflict in the political decision-making process:

(1) Pressure groups which may be national, regional or local, altruistic or self centred.

(2) The ordinary citizen, individually of little significance, collectively very powerful.

(3) Professional bodies which influence but have no power to decide.

(4) Elected representatives who decide or fail to decide.

[1] One criterion for justifiable road investment has recently been proposed by Mr. G. J. Roth who has suggested that road users should pay congestion costs for the use of roads (plus some allowance for wear and tear). Road authorities would be instructed to charge full 'user costs' in this sense and use the surplus of revenue over expenditure to improve roads where congestion remained most severe. See *A Self-financing Road System*, Research Monograph 3, IEA, 1966.

[2] W. J. M. Mackenzie, 'Administrative Aspects of Buchanan and Crowther,' *Journal of Town Planning Institute*, July/August 1964.

Professor Mackenzie concludes pessimistically

> '...that in any form of human government the odds are against clear choice and rational decision; we can attain these good things only partially and even then only by a great effort.'

Certainly the fact that there has been no break-through or substantial progress towards a solution since *Traffic in Towns* was first published lends support to this pessimism. But somewhere between the vagueness of past planning and the precision of the computer some progress may be possible, and the present author considers it must occur on or near the economic front and that improvement of pricing policies will necessarily play a prominent part (see Chapters 8 and 9).

Finally, on the question of choice, the Report (para. 444 quoted above) suggests that each town should decide the 'vehicular accessibility' it wishes to have and is prepared to pay for. It is fairly clear that the bulk of Buchanan's recommended expenditures, if they are to be made at all, must fall on central government (see below, pp. 72—74). On these grounds alone, freedom of choice by each individual town or city would be out of the question. Common techniques and criteria would need to be applied in different circumstances and local opinions and preferences could not legitimately be allowed over-riding weight.[1] Also with growth of travel and the ubiquity of the private car, few towns and cities can be regarded as self-contained or independent in terms of traffic.

It seems therefore that local choice on major matters such as cost (but not necessarily on lay-out details) would inevitably be small, and the implementation of Buchanan's plans would demand firm central control in the formative stages with all final decisions taken by the state.

An improbable forecast

More directly and pertinently than the comments made above, the Buchanan Report has been criticised by Professor Beesley and

---

[1] This would not of course mean that all towns and cities would have the same physical treatment. It merely means that such things as rates of return, capital costs per additional vehicle accommodated might be standardised. Within these limits variety in plans, preservation of outstanding features, and architectural freedom should give substantial variety in final solutions.

Dr J. F. Kain.[1] Amongst other things, based on American experience and data, they question the forecast of levels of car ownership in Britain, given the higher population densities common in our cities, Leeds being the particular case chosen for study. This view is confirmed by the results of the London Traffic Survey[2] (and by other data), Fig. 5—9 of which shows that an increase in net residential density from 10 to 150 persons per acre tends to reduce average car ownership for all income groups from 65 per cent to 30 per cent of households. Professor Beesley and Dr Kain therefore doubt whether the levels of car ownership forecast by Professor Buchanan for cities would take place unless there was much large-scale dispersal or decentralisation and consequent lower densities in British cities. But if this decentralisation occurred, they show that urban road construction would be less costly than assumed by Professor Buchanan. In contrast to *Traffic in Towns* they imply that at least part of the solution to urban traffic problems must lie in dispersal or decentralisation, together with road pricing and modest investment.

These comments and criticisms do not of course disprove the Buchanan thesis, assumptions or method of approach, for, to take only one point, it is not yet known how feasible it will be to disperse or to decentralise British cities; this topic will be discussed in more detail in Chapter 7. They do suggest however that the solution (or solutions) to the urban traffic problems are not yet obvious. That is to say, we do not know at all precisely how equilibrium between vehicle ownership and use, city size and city lay-out should be achieved. There are after all many possible margins on which semi-voluntary adjustments to an overall equilibrium could take place—restraint on vehicle use, restraint by congestion, traffic engineering and management, changes in user's timing and direction of travel, dispersal or decentralisation of land uses and points of attraction, or changes in modes of transport. It therefore seems likely that adjustments towards an equilibrium will take place on many margins rather than mainly on two, road investment plus restraint of traffic, as Buchanan assumed.

[1] M. E. Beesley and J. F. Kain, 'Urban Form, Car Ownership and Public Policy: An appraisal of Traffic in Towns,' *Urban Studies*, November, 1964.
[2] Freeman Fox and Partners (*et alia*), *London Traffic Survey, Vol. 1*, London County Council, 1964.

Simple future projections of urban traffic are likely to give traffic volumes well in excess of the capacity of any urban road systems that can be built for many years to come, but there is some evidence that a tolerable equilibrium at lower traffic volumes than forecast by *Traffic in Towns* will take place. Ordinary supply/ demand analysis suggests that traffic and the corresponding mean journey speeds will level off near, but not at, the point of breakdown; for almost by definition regular and expected congestion cannot become intolerable. This view is confirmed by experience in London in recent years.[1] On the other hand, stand-stills over wide areas due to some unpredictable event will probably become increasingly frequent, and such an equilibrium would be contrary to travel preferences and unlikely to endure in the long run.

SUMMARY

To summarise our preliminary appraisal, we have shown that the fundamental assumption of *Traffic in Towns*, that our towns and cities should be retained 'broadly in the present form', is self-defeating since the implied expenditure (see below, pp. 71—74) and period are such that the shape of our cities could if we wished be substantially changed. We have argued that, unlike an efficient market, the democratic political process is not sufficiently sophisticated to permit the degree of local influence which the Report proposed, the more so since the major resources would necessarily have to be provided by the central government. Moreover the forecast levels of car ownership and use on which the whole Buchanan case rests may be exaggerated and inconsistent with past and present experience. The emphasis on 'intolerable' levels of congestion would apparently imply the need for a capacity substantially in excess of any practicable road system or arbitary restraints on traffic, whilst in reality congestion is likely to settle below the point of breakdown.

Nevertheless, despite these doubts and deficiencies in its thesis, *Traffic in Towns* represents the most widely accepted approach to urban planning and traffic. It is for that reason necessary to consider the problems of applying its proposals in more detail, if only to reject them in favour of alternative solutions.

[1] R. J. Smeed, 'The Traffic Problem in Towns: A Review of Possible Long-Term Solutions', *Town Planning Review*, Vol. XXXV(2), 1964.

CHAPTER 5

TRAFFIC IN TOWNS:
PROBLEMS OF APPLICATION AND ALTERNATIVES

ECONOMIC GROWTH AND RESOURCES

A PRIOR matter in long-term planning of urban road investments and urban renewal is the future growth of national output, for economic growth seems essential if painful questions of priorities in the public sector, and the growth of the public sector *vis à vis* the private, are to be avoided or at least minimised. However there is considerable controversy and doubt about the prospects for growth, both over the past experience and on the future outlook, and, like town planning, the value of planning for growth, which implies forecasting, lies more in broadly anticipating problems and solutions than reliably indicating precise future developments.

Experience since the war seems to have been as follows. During the 1950s the output of the British economy increased at an average rate of 2.6 per cent per annum, made up of an average increase in productivity per head of 1.9 per cent per annum and an average increase in the size of the labour force of 0.7 per cent per annum.[1] Over this period however the annual rate of increase in productivity per head rose from 1.77 per cent in 1952 to 2.55 per cent in 1962. An alternative estimate has been an increase in productivity per head of 2.9 per cent in 1961-64.[2]

Since these growth rates were achieved largely before growth itself became a prime object of public policy and in view of the much higher rates of growth achieved during the 1950s by some

[1] W. A. H. Godley and J. R. Shepherd, 'Long-Term Growth and Short-Term Policy', National Institute *Economic Review*, August 1964.
[2] F. T. Blackaby, '4 per cent Again', *District Bank Review*, December 1964.

European countries, e.g. Germany with 7.6 per cent per annum,[1] the situation at one time seemed set for a long-term growth rate of 4 per cent per annum, made up of a 3 per cent increase per annum in productivity per head and an increase of perhaps 1 per cent per annum in the labour force. But it now seems this expectation was over-optimistic. The high European growth rates could be at least partly attributable to a large transfer of labour from agriculture to other higher productivity industries and occupations, a process which had already gone much further in Britain than on the Continent. Also, whilst the gross population of working age (those aged 15 to 64) is currently expected to increase by roughly 1·5 per cent per annum over the period 1964 to 2000,[2] it is unwise to assume that working habits will not change over such a long period and with such a large possible increase in output and in income per head.

Future working habits may change in three main ways: people may demand increased leisure (including longer holidays), delay their entry into the labour force because of increase in the periods of education, or they may retire earlier. Some offset to these may be provided however by an increasing tendency for women to enter, or remain, in paid work.

Growth, output and leisure
Much has been written about spectacular future reductions in working hours consequent on automation and rising standards of living, but present evidence does not bear these optimistic forecasts out. Thus average weekly hours in 1962 as compared with 1952 had only declined by about 2.5 per cent or by 0.3 per cent per annum.[3] An increase in the average period of education of two years by the end of the century, and an average of two years' earlier retirement would reduce the gross population of working age by about 10 per cent by the end of the century, again a reduction of about 0.3 per cent per annum. These changes could in effect partly cancel out future increase in working population.

In sum then, in spite of the uncertainties and short-term difficulties and fluctuations, it seems that an average annual growth rate of

[1] A. C. L. Day, 'The Myth of 4 per cent Growth', *Westminster Bank Review*, November 1964.
[2] *Annual Abstract of Statistics 1965*, HMSO, 1966.
[3] National Institute *Economic Review*, Statistical Appendix, August 1964.

3 per cent might be attainable in the long run and, compared with the 3.8 per cent assumed for the National Plan, seems a reasonable working estimate for future planning.[1] The 3 per cent rate implies almost a trebling of output and a doubling of real income per head by the end of the century as compared with 1964.

It is difficult to be accurate but estimates of growth for the economy as a whole and for individual sectors should at the very least be consistent. For example it is commonly held that we may look forward to a three- or two-day working week by the end of the century, yet it is also believed that we will be unable to 'afford' the expenditure required to carry out road investment, urban renewal and other expenditures in the public sector. Although our economic and political systems may work somewhat imperfectly and irrationally, is it not unlikely that people will choose to take greatly increased amounts of leisure, presumably because of increased prosperity, yet be unable or unwilling to arrange their affairs and government so as to meet those demands which are considered pressing and 'essential'?

THE COST OF THE BUCHANAN PROPOSALS

The other major question in trying to carry out the recommendations of the Buchanan Report is the cost of its proposals and the problems of obtaining the necessary volume of resources by which to carry them out.

In the Buchanan Report only a few estimates were made of the cost of the proposals and they are therefore difficult to expand to give national totals. The £4½ million estimate for Newbury and the £90 million estimate for Leeds can be expanded on a per capita basis to give an estimate of £4,500 million for primary networks for all towns in England and Wales of population over 50,000 and might perhaps be increased by 25—50 per cent to cover the necessary subsidiary and distributory roads, that is, £5,500 million to £6,500 million. But Professor Buchanan now admits that his estimates were too low, and if in addition they are expanded to cover towns of over 10,000 the total capital cost may be of the order of £10,000 million at 1963 prices, and these would even so

[1] A cautious planner would of course work out the implications for his plans of alternative rates of economic growth rather than rely on a single target which might not be achieved.

imply some restraint on traffic, in the cities at least.

Other responsible estimates have been higher than this. For example Mr C. D. Foster[1] estimated a total of £18,000[2] million and in view of the normal almost inevitable tendencies to under-estimate costs and for the solution of one problem to uncover another (e.g. bottle-necks) it would be unwise to regard this estimate as too high. It seems therefore that the road investments implied by Buchanan will cost something of the order of £10,000 million to £20,000 million. Because of the difficulties in estimating costs before detailed proposals are made it would be foolish to go into more detail at this stage. Of these estimates a proportion, perhaps up to one-third, would consist of land costs which would impose no necessary burden on the current resources of the economy (see page 55 and footnote). But old property acquired to build roads will be replaced by new at higher cost in both money and real terms so that, with some element of improvement included, urban road expenditure will possibly represent the real strain on resources.

In spite of the uncertainties, it seems unlikely that the total cost of the Buchanan approach for towns over, say, 10,000 will be less than about £20,000 million, and it is by no means clear why small towns should either be excluded or given low priority. The problems are certainly greatest in the larger towns and cities and conurbations, but so are the costs; the balance between benefits and costs would not necessarily favour the larger towns and cities.

As an order of magnitude therefore one can assume an investment in urban road networks of at least £20,000 million at present prices. Spread over 40 years this sum would require an average urban road investment of £500 million a year compared with about £50 million per annum in 1963-64, and a projected expenditure of £150 million per annum in 1970-71 (or about half projected road investment in that year). *The Buchanan approach implies that we should sacrifice an additional £350 million to £450 million a year which would be otherwise devoted to other things.*

[1] C. D. Foster, 'Estimates of the Cost of Buchanan,' *The Statist*, 24 February, 1964.

[2] A further independent estimate (as yet unpublished) by the National Institute of Economic and Social Research is broadly comparable. It calculates a total expenditure on all transport modernisation needs, road, rail, ports, etc., of £25,000 to £30,000 million in the next 40 years.

These resources could be made available voluntarily by increased savings (and borrowing by the relevant authorities) or compulsorily by increased revenue from taxation. It is unlikely that voluntary savings would increase sufficiently to cover the additional urban road investment (and all other increases in investment that are 'required') so that any increased borrowing would have to be at the expense of other forms of investment which may be equally or more urgent.[1]

The required resources would therefore have to be diverted from other uses by local or central taxation. Since local authorities would in practice have the major tasks and decisions in implementing the Buchanan Report, in principle there would be something to be said for the burden falling on ratepayers. But this proposal would be quite impossible to implement at present because revenue from rates—the local authorities' principal independent source—is only some £1,100 million per annum.[2] Furthermore rates have several drawbacks as a tax: they are regressive (bearing most heavily on the lowest incomes[3]), inflexible and difficult to raise, with none of the natural buoyancy of central government revenue in a period of inflation and of rising real income. Also rates are in effect a tax on development and an increase in rates is hardly likely to encourage urban re-development and urban renewal by private developers.

In practice therefore it seems that the major part of the cost will inevitably fall on central government sources of revenue. Although any arrangements made would need to establish a reasonable degree of participation and responsibility by the local authority, the present road grant system whereby 75, 60 and 50 per cent of capital costs for Class I, II and III roads respectively are borne by central government, might be satisfactory for this purpose.

An estimate of the financial/budgetary problem of the public

---

[1] As indicated in Chapter 1 borrowing (as compared with taxation) does not reduce the real burden of a given investment on the economy in terms of current resources, although it does make it voluntary rather than compulsory. Nor of course will road tolls or pricing necessarily provide the resources to build extra roads on any scale.

[2] *Annual Abstract of Statistics*, 1965, *op. cit.*,

[3] Social Survey, 'The Impact of Taxes and Social Service Benefits on Different Groups of Households', *Economic Trends*, November 1962.

sector (central and local government) over the period 1964-70 has been set down in *The National Plan*.[1] Public expenditure is already expected to increase at the rate of 4¼ per cent per annum, in excess of the optimistic growth rate of 3.8 per cent per annum for the economy assumed in the Plan. Road investment, which is planned to increase by 10 per cent per annum (constant prices) from 1964-70 is in a strong position in the budgetary sense, because the growth of traffic will itself provide extra central government revenue and command over real resources without a rise in rates of taxation. Nevertheless for want of any obvious guides to the proper relationship between public expenditure and GNP, there is a strong tendency by the Treasury to try to hold the ratio down as a method of control.

Could we afford Buchanan?

The *National Plan* has suggested that there will be rising demands and severe strain on the building and construction industry up to 1970. Fortunately the road construction sector of the industry employs the more 'efficient' and larger firms which can probably expand most easily and use least man-power per £ of construction. But expansion will nevertheless be difficult in the immediate future; labour may prove the main bottleneck and, significantly, road construction costs rose by 9 per cent from 1962 to 1964.

In the longer run however the allocation of adequate resources is likely to be easier. Starting from a possible base expenditure of £150 million in 1970, an annual rate of increase of about 5 per cent per annum in urban road investment would cover a £20,000 million expenditure (at present prices) in about 40 years and a 10 per cent rate of increase would cover the same expenditure in about 27 years. With our progressive system of taxation (particularly motor taxation) and assuming a 3 per cent annual rate of growth of GNP, this expenditure could be carried out with no increase in current rates of taxation,[2] *provided the remainder of public expenditure does not increase much more rapidly than national output.*

[1] Department of Economic Affairs, *The National Plan*, Cmnd. 2764, HMSO, 1965.
[2] Progressive taxation implies that an increasing proportion of a rising GNP will be collected by government.

Our calculations thus assume that this level of public expenditure will not have other undesirable economic consequences which could frustrate the assumed rate of growth of GNP, that taxpayers will be prepared to hand over a rising proportion of income to the government and that increases in other government expenditure (on, say, education or hospitals) do not rise much faster than the rate of growth of GNP. Whether or not these three conditions are likely to obtain over a period of 40 years is of course far from certain. But with these provisos we can show that it is possible to finance the Buchanan programme—*not* that it is justified.

	5 per cent annual rate of increase	10 per cent annual rate of increase
1970—9	£1,900 million	£2,400 million
1980—9	£3,100 million	£6,200 million
1990—9	£5,000 million	£16,200 million
2000—9	£8,200 million	

Total 1970—2009 £18,200 ,, Total 1970—99 £24,800 ,,

The suggested rate of growth of urban road expenditure, 5—10 per cent per annum, is still substantially above the likely future rate of growth of the whole economy which, more modestly than the expectations of the National Plan, seems unlikely to exceed 3 per cent per annum in the long run. But the problem must be placed in perspective. At a 3 per cent rate of growth gross national product can be expected to increase from about £29,000 million in 1964 to about £84,000 million in 2000 (at 1964 prices) and to £130,000 million in 2010. The growth in real income per head and in population, which are part causes of the problem Buchanan was set to tackle (motoring expenditure and revenue are increasing more rapidly than income per head) could in the long run provide the resources in the public sector to implement the *Traffic in Towns* proposals.

In the long-run programme listed above, the capacity of the building industry should rise sufficiently to provide the required resources, but one major problem remains. Buchanan estimates that half the increase to the so-called 'ultimate' volume of traffic will have taken place by 1973 whereas half the £20,000 million road expenditure listed above will only have taken place by about 2000 in the case of the 5 per cent programme and by about 1990 in the case of the 10 per cent programme, a time-lag of 17 to 27 years. But other demands on the required physical resources and output such as defence, education, housing, hospitals, are also pressing, some perhaps more urgently than urban roads and renewal. One of the major problems in public finance is the enormous difficulty of establishing objective criteria for the allocation of public expenditure.

It is not possible that tax-financed urban road investment can match the projected increases in urban traffic in the near future, and the outlook is therefore one of early congestion, restrictions and traffic management (from which considerable gains can be expected)[1] accompanied by urban road investment which could rise to a rate of about £850 million to £2,000 million a year by the end of the century. There are several other reasons indicating a time-table of this kind. Traffic surveys cannot be carried out and analysed in less than about two years, and the drawing up and approval of plans and the acquisition of the necessary land and property both take a similar period: the time-lag from conception to start of construction is thus at least six years. And we have still assumed that the intellectual and technical problems of urban planning are solved and that there will be no staffing shortages.

The implementation of Buchanan and urban renewal policies thus demand a virtual revolution in planning if not in the rôle of government. New techniques would have to be evolved, learnt and taught and since mistakes are likely it would be as well if expenditure in the early years was relatively small.

To sum up then, some formidable problems in planning, policy, phasing and priorities would have to be faced in carrying out substantial urban road investments but in the long run, given reasonable economic growth, the resources to carry out such

---

[1] The conflict between traffic management schemes and the 'environment' predicted in *Traffic in Towns* is by no means certain to take place. To take a well-known London scheme, the improvement of the environment in Tottenham Court Road probably compensates for its worsening in Gower Street. Also bottlenecks on main routes encourage traffic to detour through residential areas, worsening the environment, and their elimination would improve it.

proposals should not be one of them. End-century plans for urban road investment of about £400 per head of present city populations could be attained.

But the use of resources on such a scale would demand continuing economic justification, and even accepting the Buchanan thesis as *the* answer to urban traffic and planning problems, this condition would be hard to fulfil. It is important, however, that immediate difficulties in solving the urban traffic problem or in securing increased resources for road investment should not inhibit realistic planning and research. Quite apart from the urban traffic problem, Britain is facing a substantial increase in urban population and a massive investment in urban expansion and renewal is inevitable.[1] Not to try to plan this expansion adequately and realistically would be dangerous. It is all too easy to fall into a vicious circle: developments are not planned because resources are not made available and resources are not made available because sound planning has not been done. To break this circle, realistic analysis and research into solutions to urban planning problems are required.

CHOICE OF PLANNING PERIOD

Before considering the application of *Traffic in Towns* in more detail, an important question to be decided is how far we can look ahead in terms of traffic volumes and planning.

Buchanan envisages a period for transportation plans of

'up to the end of the century or a little beyond, this being the period in which the great bulk of the development of motor traffic is likely to take place . . . Major road works are so costly and so difficult to alter once they have been executed that it seems essential to visualise the long-term requirements'.[2]

Other factors appear to reinforce this view. One is the magnitude of total expenditure and another is the need to ensure that short-term plans and proposals lie on the path towards a final solution. With a 3 per cent growth rate in the output of the building industry devoted to housing it should be possible to consider replacing almost all the housing at present in existence, by the end of the

---

[1] P. A. Stone, 'Urban Development and National Resources', *Urban Studies*, November 1964.

[2] *Op. cit.*, paras. 449 and 450.

century (see Chapter 6), and such a programme might offer opportunities for radical improvement in our cities. Finally the intellectual, administrative and practical problems which implementing Buchanan and re-shaping our towns raise, are bound to take a long time to resolve. Apparently a long planning period is again indicated.

Yet other factors militate against the extremely long period advocated by Buchanan. One is obvious: it is difficult to forecast even broad lines of development over such a long period,[1] particularly when income per head will possibly double or working and leisure habits change. The possibility of forecasting in any detail is proportionately less. Again, Buchanan chooses such a long period, partly because he envisages that saturation-level in traffic will be reached by about the end of the century or a little beyond—which may perhaps be true of vehicles per head of population but is unlikely to be true of total population if only because the most fertile age groups (ages 20—39) are expected to increase more rapidly than total population up to the end of the century.[2]

Finally, working to a long-term plan to be fully implemented in 40 years' time carries with it the danger of inhibiting shorter-term developments which are inconsistent with the plan, yet which might otherwise be worthwhile. Over a 40-year planning period, the plan will be such a vague and uncertain long-term objective that interim plans and changes will be absolutely essential. The cumulative effect of such changes is likely to be such as to invalidate the original conception of the plan.

In addition to the problem of the length of planning period, questions as to the proper phasing of the work on road construction and urban renewal will arise. Do we work on all towns simultaneously, gradually carrying out the work in each town over the next 40 or so years or do we work on each town in turn intensively for a few years? Here all the relevant factors—the distribution of building capacity, the need for re-housing of persons displaced by

[1] Some of these problems are discussed and illustrated in John Brunner, *The National Plan: a preliminary assessment*, Eaton Paper 4, second edition, IEA, 1965, and in Duncan Burn, John Seale, A. R. N. Ratcliff, *Lessons from Central Forecasting*, Eaton Paper 6, IEA, 1965.

[2] *Annual Abstract of Statistics*, 1965, *op. cit.*

urban renewal, and the avoidance of severe dislocation—point to the gradual alternative, which again favours a long planning period. But on the whole a long-term plan seems only just worthwhile and then only because it might indicate broad future problems and solutions; detailed projections and plans over such a long period can be of little or no value.[1]

OPTIONAL TRAFFIC—METHODS OF RESTRICTION

Turning to consider the central question of optional traffic it must be remembered that Buchanan in his preamble[2] considered that 'it is reasonable to suppose that towns and cities will continue to exist broadly in their present form'. This conclusion was based partly on matters of fact and conjecture such as past history and possible future developments, and partly on what was considered desirable, for example, the avoidance of urban spread.

Within this broad assumption Buchanan analysed growth in terms of traffic essential 'to service and maintain the life of a community' and optional traffic:

'the traffic arising from the exercise of a choice to use a vehicle for a journey when the option existed either not to make the journey at all or to make it by some other kind of vehicle or form of transport'.[3]

Professor Buchanan admits that it is not always possible to differentiate between the two, and indeed there are very substantial philosophical and administrative difficulties in doing so. Is it possible to prove that car use on a commuting trip is less important than, say, on a shopping trip?

[1] The distinction between a projection and a plan is broadly similar to that between a forecast and a target. The two are often confused. Thus it is not always possible, even with a document of the importance of *The National Plan*, to say whether the figures refer to what will happen (forecasts) or what *ought* to, or what the government believes should, occur (target). The distinction is always difficult to apply in practice because forecasts cannot be made in abstraction from assumed policies. But it is nonetheless fundamental and the customary procedure of ignoring it frustrates analysis of policy and reinforces the danger that policies will be based on misreadings of the data on which they were founded.
[2] *Op. cit.*, para. 58.
[3] *Op. cit.*, Appendix 3.

From his analysis of case studies, he argued that future growth of peak-hour traffic could not be absorbed, either physically or at tolerable cost, in the centres of Norwich, Leeds and London. Restrictions on the level of optional traffic would, he thought, be necessary and there was a choice of methods—control by category of traffic or of use, by pricing, by parking policy or by subsidisation of public transport. Thus for a given town we have inter-related choices amongst methods of restriction, degrees of restriction and cost of re-development with the aim of obtaining the optimum lay-out and the optimum quantity and composition of traffic. But such optimum decisions are in practice extraordinarily difficult to take.

It is clear from the Buchanan analysis and from the general nature of the traffic problem that the degree of restriction on 'optional' traffic required will vary from zero on the outskirts of cities where traffic is light and/or road capacity high (or easily raised) to an unknown degree in town centres. This condition must be borne in mind when considering alternative methods of restriction, the most important of which are now discussed.

(1)   *Restriction by category of traffic or of uses*
Accepting Buchanan's categories of use for the sake of argument, industrial, commercial, shopping and public transport trips are 'essential' to the operation of the town centre 'in its present form' and should therefore be accommodated. Car commuter traffic is then the residual option. As a policy it might be decided to provide road capacity and other facilities to accommodate all business and shopping plus, say, 50 per cent of optional traffic. But the problem would then be to ensure that the road capacity would only be used by the traffic for which it was designed. Although there seems an attractive simplicity in proposing to design the road system to accommodate 'appropriate' proportions of different categories of traffic, the problem would be to *identify* the categories and enforce restrictions to exclude traffic categories for which the future system had not been designed. How can one *distinguish* commuting from a business journey or shopping trip? How can one prevent one while permitting the other?[1] Some simple indiscriminate

---

[1] Indeed a commuter by car can also be (or claim to be) a traveller on business or a shopper.

method of control, at least applicable to car traffic, the most 'expensive' or 'spacious' user of scarce road space, would therefore be necessary.

(2) Restriction by road pricing

Pricing, to cover the difference between the private and social costs[1] of car travel in congested (or potentially congestible) areas, is a less arbitrary system of control and would tend to bear heavily— or could be applied exclusively—to car traffic. Three broad methods of pricing are available, a fixed charge to enter a particular area, a fixed surcharge on parking, and direct charging by electronic device.

The fixed charge for entry has the advantage of simplicity but can raise serious problems at the boundaries and cannot provide the more precise variation in degree of restriction which was demanded by Buchanan and is required for the efficient control of congestion. Parking surcharges and charges via electronic devices can to some extent overcome these difficulties.[2] Further advantages of pricing systems are that explicit decisions on 'permissible' volumes and types of traffic are unnecessary and that local revenues can be used to indicate the scale of road investment required to satisfy demand. In spite of their potential superiority over other systems of control, at the time of writing, they require further development and experimental application, but with determination there is little doubt that practicable systems could be devised.

(3) Parking restrictions

Control of traffic volumes might be obtained by restricting the total amount of parking space, siting it in such a way that the proportion of total traffic encouraged to stop and park is progressively increased towards the town centre[3] or so that certain users are encouraged

---

[1] The distinction between private and social costs is briefly described and discussed on pp. 12—13 and 31—41.

[2] Although electronic devices need more development whilst restraint by parking surcharges encourages the growth of non-parking traffic in town centres. However the latter drawback might be overcome by providing ring routes for through traffic of such high capacity and attraction that the existing road system in town centres is not used by through traffic to any extent. See *Road Pricing: the Economic and Technical Possibilities*, HMSO, 1964.

[3] W. G. Smigielski *et alia*, *Leicester Traffic Plan*, City of Leicester, October 1964.

and others discouraged. These alternatives are not mutually exclusive.

As traffic volumes increase towards the town centre, parking space could be designed to 'intercept' an increasing proportion of traffic. The problem here is the question of enforcement and/or incentives to encourage vehicle occupants to park and (say) continue their journey by public transport. Park and ride schemes are often proposed, the car driver being given a subsidised rate on public transport on production of a parking ticket[1] and indeed strong enforcement and proper pricing might ensure that such parking space as was provided would in fact be used, at least towards the town centre. However, enforcement over a wide area would be difficult[2] and space in the various parks might tend to be allocated to commuters on the basis of 'first come first served' rather than on 'importance of journey' or ability to pay. (See Appendix on Parking Policy, p. 94.)

(4) *Private restriction by subsidy to public transport*

Subsidisation of the bus is often recommended because of divergences between private and social costs and the space-saving characteristics of public transport. The aim is to make public transport attractive *vis à vis* the private car. But except in the special case of London where size, distance and population make frequent and fast train services (surface and underground) possible, there are fundamental reasons why public transport cannot compete in speed, frequency and convenience with the private car if competition is on equal terms. Whilst the private car can operate to the convenience of one or a few persons only (at a private running cost comparable to bus fares) the bus, in order to get reasonable occupancy, must operate infrequently or stop frequently and is thus at a fundamental disadvantage. This disadvantage is least where population densities and traffic congestion are highest, but it nevertheless remains.

The problems of encouraging public transport *vis à vis* the car can be highlighted in the following way. In Central London the average journey time per mile (straight line distance) on a sample

[1] Although an experiment in 'park and ride' in Leeds in mid-1965, whereby car drivers were charged 1s. 6d. for peripheral parking and for a 3-mile return bus trip, was not attractive and was abandoned.

[2] Consider the problems of provision of parking space for residents.

of journeys was 5.8 minutes per mile by car, but 9.5 minutes for bus travel plus 9.9 minutes walking and waiting time.[1] From this it can be calculated that, assuming running costs of 4d. per mile by car, a car owner would still prefer the use of a car to *free* bus transport on a 3-mile journey if he valued his time at more than 1s. 6d. per hour. Since the mean household income for car-owning families in London (1962) was some £1,600[2] (or some 16s. per working hour for the head of household), if car owners value their travel time at anything like their working time the inference is obvious.[3]

Scarcity of parking space, parking charges, terminal parking and walking time could narrow the advantage of the car, but probably not eliminate it.

A discriminate subsidy in the form of free travel to motorists parking on the periphery seems the only possible way in which public transport can be made more attractive *vis a vis* the private car directly, although preference for buses on the road, for example by exclusive allocation of lanes, might help if practical difficulties could be overcome. The fact must be faced however that the gap between the speed and convenience of public transport and the private car (outside London) is so large that general subsidy to public transport in a car-owning society seems unlikely to make any substantial impact. The competitive position of public transport is therefore likely to worsen. Only road pricing is likely to be able to reverse the cumulative process of transfer from bus to car in urban transport.

At present none of these alternative methods of restriction look entirely satisfactory, although for the most promising in principle, road pricing, practical schemes can be devised. With development and experimental application over the next few years, they could provide a satisfactory answer, not only to the problem of traffic restriction but to urban traffic and planning problems generally.

---

[1] E. M. Holroyd and D. A. Scraggs, 'Journey by Car and Bus in Central London', *Traffic Engineering and Control*, July 1964.

[2] Freeman Fox and Partners, *London Traffic Survey*, Vol. 1, London County Council, 1964.

[3] Professor M. E. Beesley has suggested that commuters value their travelling time at about one-third their wage rate. See 'The Value of Time Spent in Travelling: Some New Evidence', *Economica*, May 1965.

Factors affecting choice of travel mode

In a further search for indicators as to the proportions of optional traffic to be accommodated, the question of 'modal' split is examined. It can be done in many ways as many of the factors involved are inter-related.

The main 'independent' or 'semi-independent' influences which affect the choice between public and private transport for journeys to a central area (the critical point) are three:

(1)   Car ownership which is itself dependent on income, residential density, etc.[1] Even in London with a very well developed public transport system, the London Traffic Survey has shown that in car-owning households 34.5 per cent of person-journeys to the central area are made by private car[2] (as driver or passenger) and 61 per cent by mass public transport (bus, underground, British Railways). The corresponding percentages for non car-owning households are 2.2 per cent and 92 per cent. In addition, car-owning households generate more journeys per head to the central area, for although they only account for 38 per cent of all households they made 49 per cent of all journeys by all modes of transport in the central area. Thus even in Central London the car-owning household generates about 25 times the number of car journeys (occurring wholly or partly within the central area) as the non-car-owning household.

(2)   The frequency and convenience of public transport, convenience being measured by journey-time per mile which in turn is affected by speeds and by distance between origin and destination on the one hand, and the respective public transport routes, and their stopping points, on the other. Absence of changing and waiting times are also important.

(3)   Congestion and lack of parking space.

These three factors, and particularly the latter two, are correlated with many others, in particular with population density and size of population; a fairly close inverse relationship between percentage of journeys to work carried out by car, and town or city population

[1] Freeman Fox and Partners, *op. cit.*, Table 6—4B.
[2] For the critical journey to work, however, cars accounted for only about 12 per cent of those made to the central area.

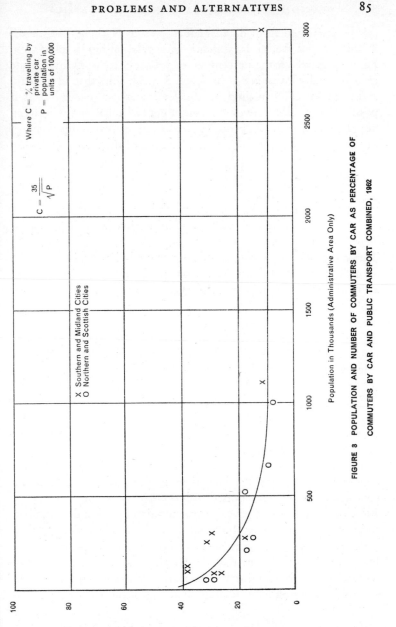

FIGURE 8   POPULATION AND NUMBER OF COMMUTERS BY CAR AS PERCENTAGE OF
COMMUTERS BY CAR AND PUBLIC TRANSPORT COMBINED, 1962

can be calculated from data obtained by the National Institute of Economic and Social Research.[1] This relationship is plotted in Figure 3 in which the percentage of journeys to work by private car is generally lower in northern and Scottish cities than in midland and southern cities, mainly because of lower car ownership. It is possible to establish however a rough general relationship between population (of the main central administrative area) and percentage of journeys to work by private car in 1962 of the form

$$C = \frac{35}{\sqrt{P}} \quad ,$$

where C=per cent of journeys to work by private car and
        P=population of main administration area in units of 100,000.

Thus a city with a population of 100,000 could be expected to have about 35 per cent of journeys to work made by private car in 1962, a city of 200,000 25 per cent, a city of 400,000 17½ per cent and so on.

Urban concentration versus dispersal

This background discussion of alternative methods of traffic restriction has not led to any obvious proposals affecting expenditure on roads, despite the fact that we must be prepared to accommodate a possible trebling of car ownership by the year 2000. It may therefore be more profitable to consider decentralised solutions to the problems posed by the growth of traffic. We should then have to consider each major traffic attractor to assess the prospects of dispersing it.

The trends towards concentration in towns may at first sight appear so strong, and the incentives to dispersal so weak, that a consideration of decentralised solutions may seem superfluous. But closer examination reveals some trends towards a decentralised pattern of urban living, both inside and outside existing urban areas, and it would be dangerous to ignore them (see Chapter 7). It is important therefore that decentralised town centre solutions should at least be considered. As shown above (Chapter 4), even a modest decentralisation such as a halving of the working popula-

[1] G. F. Ray and R. E. Crum, 'Transport: Notes and Comments', NIESR *Economic Review*, May 1963.

tion (area staying the same) or a doubling of the central area (working population staying the same) can make a substantial difference. One solution to the town centre problem is a terminal 'ring' or 'box' road, widely drawn, which would encourage dispersal of central attractors in the long run,[1] as well as encouraging traffic to avoid the town centre. At some cost in additional vehicle mileage a square grid lay-out (in contrast to a radial road system) can be shown to lessen the central concentration of traffic[2] and thus further to encourage dispersal of central attractors.

THE ENVIRONMENTAL AREA

The idea of an environmental area proposed by Professor Buchanan is aimed at safeguarding the 'environment' in more or less self-contained residential areas by excluding extraneous traffic[3] and directing it onto a specialised road distributor network where traffic is dominant. The analogy is with rooms where 'environment' and non-transport activities are dominant, and corridors where transport and traffic are dominant.

Although the concept of the environmental area seems excellent it has not previously been fully analysed and it is in consequence difficult to apply. In his detailed proposals[4] Buchanan seems to be aiming at a Radburn-type lay-out[5] on the existing street system, aiming at excluding extraneous traffic by road closure. Since the aim of the environmental area is to reduce vehicle mileage within it (ignoring any additional vehicle mileage that occurs outside it) the closure of a road seems worth while when through traffic vehicle mileage excluded from the area is more than the additional vehicle mileage forced on traffic with origins and/or destinations within the area. But one must take account of the possibility that the 'internal' increase in vehicle mileage may be so large that road closures may result in a net increase in vehicle mileage and a worsening of the environment in Professor Buchanan's own terms. In practice, without very detailed knowledge of the origins and

---

[1] W. G. Smigielski, *op. cit.*
[2] H. T. Fisher and N. M. Boukidis, 'Consequences of Obliquity in Arterial Street Systems', *Traffic Quarterly*, January 1963.
[3] Traffic with no origin or destination within the area.
[4] *Op. cit.*, Fig. 137.
[5] *Op. cit.*, Figs. 61 and 62.

destinations of traffic and their chosen routes, it is probably impossible to discover whether a particular road closure will reduce or increase traffic within the area, and consequently whether it will improve or worsen the environment. To clarify the meaning and application of the concept of the environmental area it must be further analysed towards its logical conclusion—the minimisation of *total* traffic (more precisely vehicle mileage) within the area. It should be noted that this objective is very different from that of those who advocate the use of road pricing, the chief aim of which is to ensure that traffic pays the full costs of road use without prejudging the question of how much traffic there should be.

Ring versus direct routing

If the object is to minimise total vehicle mileage and its adverse effects on environment within the area, the concept evolved by Dr R. J. Smeed[1] of ring routing (illustrated in Figure 4) becomes relevant. Under this scheme traffic with destinations within the area travels on a ring road (or the distributor network) round the circumference of an area (assumed to be circular) until it reaches the radial routes (or whatever access actually exists) on which their destinations lie. It then travels along the radii to its destination. By insisting on the maximum travel on the outer ring, vehicle mileage within the area tends to be minimised.

To illustrate the effects let us assume a circular environmental area with an infinite number of radial accesses and show average distances for ring routing (Fig. 4) and direct routing (Fig. 5) respectively for the three separate kinds of journey. These types are (i) internal journeys (wholly within the area), (ii) cross-cordon journeys (from or to the area to and from outside), and (iii) through journeys (journeys that would normally pass through the area). They are illustrated in Figs. 4 and 5. Assuming journeys between random points for all three types, the average length of all possible journeys in terms of the radius of the environmental area (r) is given in Table VI.

The absolute values for direct and for ring routing will of course be affected by the actual road network within the area and the form

[1] R. J. Smeed, 'The Traffic Problem in Towns,' Manchester Statistical Society, 8 February, 1961.

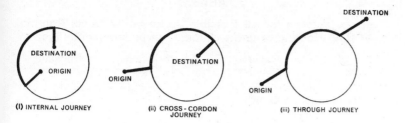

FIGURE 4   RING ROUTING ILLUSTRATED FOR INTERNAL JOURNEYS,
CROSS-CORDON JOURNEYS AND THROUGH JOURNEYS

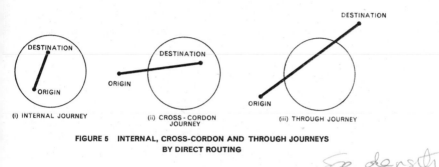

FIGURE 5   INTERNAL, CROSS-CORDON AND THROUGH JOURNEYS
BY DIRECT ROUTING

of ring routing chosen. The *ratios* between direct and ring routing
will be much less affected, however.

Ring routing, therefore, as opposed to direct routing, increases
the average mileage of through journeys least and that of
internal journeys most. Similarly the average savings of internal
distance from ring routing are higher for through journeys
and lower for internal journeys. The total effect of substituting ring
routing for direct routing will depend on the proportions of through
journeys, cross-cordon journeys, and internal journeys. These
three in turn depend on the size of the area; the bigger the area,
the less will be the proportion of through trips. If there are equal
proportions of the three types of journey and all journeys are
random, direct routing will give an average journey length of
1.10r (all within the environmental area) and ring routing will
give instead an average journey length of 1.90r of which 0.33r

TABLE VI

Average Distance for All Possible Journeys by Direct Routing and Ring Routing in terms of radius of environmental area r

Routing	Internal Journeys	Cross-Cordon Journeys	Through Journeys
Direct (all mileage within area)	0·90r	1·13r	1·27r
External ring (mileage within area in brackets)	2·24r (0·67r)	1·90 (0·33r)	1·57r (0)

will take place inside the area. To save a vehicle mile in the environmental area, roughly two vehicle miles must take place outside it; is this price worth paying to protect the environment and how is ring routing to be enforced?

The above analysis implies the closure of streets at the centre of the environmental area and the maintenance of maximum outward access to the external ring; but this will have very serious effects on certain journeys. For through journeys the worst consequence will be that a journey of 2r through the environmental area will be converted into a journey of 3.14r around the ring. But a cross-cordon journey of little more than r within the area will be converted into a journey of almost 4.14r, of which almost r will take place inside the area. Finally a very short direct journey between an origin and destination near the centre of the environmental area could be converted into a journey of as much as 5.14r, almost 2r of which might have to be made within the area. Although the *average* savings given in Table VI would be achieved by ring routing supported by road closures at the centre to enforce it, the effects on some individual journeys, houses and families (in loss of access) *is so serious as to throw doubt on the acceptability of the proposal*.

One proposed remedy is that the environmental area concept should be applied mainly by making the external ring and distributor network very attractive to traffic in terms of design, capacity and speed, and by making journeys through the environmental area less attractive. Two methods are possible: first, by designing and sign-posting the intersections on the distributor network to make journeys through the environmental area more difficult or less attractive or, second, by reducing the capacity of the highway system inside the environmental area, either by narrowing the roads, thus increasing their environmental capacity in Buchanan's terminology[1] but reducing their traffic capacity, or by priority devices for pedestrians which would tend also to discourage motorists. Since through traffic in particular would tend to avoid such an area the concept suggested for the environmental area will resemble that proposed by Buchanan, but without road closures, and with more direct means for giving preference to the pedestrian and the environment.

Other problems of the application of environmental areas remain. For example, how far should or can they be adapted to natural groupings that may already exist such as neighbourhoods, or the catchment areas of schools or local shopping centres?[2] Defining environmental areas will be facilitated to some extent if the primary road network to carry the major traffic flows is designed first. But even this simplified analysis shows that both in their principles and in their application they are more complex than *Traffic in Towns* indicated. A lot more work remains to be done on what may ultimately prove a valuable concept, at least in those situations where traffic and environment are obviously and seriously in conflict.

At the present time it is neither possible to judge how wide and serious this conflict is, nor whether the concept of the environmental area should be applied universally or only in special situations. Surprisingly, no research or cost-benefit analyses seem to have been undertaken to estimate for instance whether the avoidance of noise or delay to perhaps only a very few people justifies the many possible extra vehicle miles that are implied.

---

[1] *Op. cit.*, p. 203.

[2] From the town planning and traffic point of view there is much to be said for designing or adapting lay-outs to reflect natural groupings. The crucial questions are whether existing towns, having grown somewhat haphazardly, can be so adapted, and whether in a highly mobile age the idea of a fairly self-contained neighbourhood is realistic.

CONCLUSIONS AND ALTERNATIVES

Although one cannot but admire the imaginative contributions of Professor Buchanan and his team, closer inspection has revealed serious doubts. This attempt to apply the proposals of *Traffic in Towns* has revealed gaps which have not been filled by subsequent work or developments.

Though the concept of the environmental area seems valuable and is likely to endure, it was inadequately analysed in the report and its application remains somewhat obscure. Moreover, although in the long run adequate resources for substantial road investment (assuming that it is justified) could conceivably be made available if alternatives were sacrificed, the concept of optional traffic and the questions of what proportion to accommodate by road investment or eliminate by restraint seem nonetheless insoluble. It is virtually impossible to prove that one form of traffic is more important than another in the long run, or to identify the various categories in practice, and the only satisfactory method of restraint and encouragement to public transport is therefore by road pricing in which the motorist himself assesses the value, and pays the full costs, of particular trips. But under road pricing the concept of optional traffic is superfluous.

Equally seriously there is no reason to believe that in the absence of a charging system a solution will appear on the expenditure side; resources cannot be provided by rhetorical statements on the impossibility of accommodating hypothetical estimates of future traffic volumes; and it is by no means certain that these will occur. Nor incidentally do alarmist predictions of widespread and inevitable disaster to the economy if roads are not built help; significantly such statements are not made by economists in or out of the transport field. The only non-arbitrary tool for determining the proportions of traffic to be accommodated or restrained, and for solving the intellectual and quantitative problems associated with them, seems to be road pricing the practical obstacles to which can be overcome with determination and the growing realisation that no alternative of comparable efficiency and simplicity exists.

In Chapters 7 and 8 alternatives to the Buchanan approach are put forward but a brief summary may be useful at this juncture. The broad solution to the urban traffic and planning problems seems to lie in dispersal of population, housing, industry and traffic on a national, regional, and local scale. To some extent this is already happening, but neither current trends nor planning powers are sufficiently strong to secure an adequate degree of dispersal and new measures, such as road pricing and pay-roll taxes, will be necessary to impart the necessary incentives.

Locally, ring roads should be built to disperse central areas and relieve congestion, to which may be added road pricing and, towards the end of the century, the creation of environmental areas and construction of central road grids where they are justified.[1] In short if there is a general answer to the town planning and traffic problem it will be in terms of dispersal, road pricing, ring roads, central road grids and environmental areas.

[1] See footnote 1, p. 65.

APPENDIX

PARKING POLICY

ALTHOUGH parking policy does not necessarily play a large part in the Buchanan approach it is sufficiently important to warrant special discussion. Two aspects are of importance: (i) parking policy itself and (ii) estimates of the quantitative demand for parking in town centres and in residential areas for the purposes of town planning.

Two broad alternative solutions are open for the critical town centre parking problem:

(1) The conventional 'administrative' approach, as exemplified in a bulletin on parking in town centres,[1] which differentiates and discriminates between classes of parking. Commercial vehicles ('operational' parking) on the one hand are regarded as 'important', and cars ('non-operational' parking) on the other are not. It draws further distinction between the short-term and long-term parker. Special provisions for each class of parker are suggested together with time restrictions on long-term parking. Though charges are often considered, they tend to be conventional and low, rather than 'economic'; that is, they do not balance supply and demand in the short run, nor cover *current* costs of parking provision including the current market price for land in the longer run. Historical costs which merely reflect the price level at which the land happened to be acquired in the past are not directly relevant to the problem of allocating scarce parking space *now*.

(2) The economic approach, which is much simpler and less arbitrary, accepts the simple common-sense view that there is no obvious social reason to treat the allocation of parking

[1] Ministry of Housing and Local Government, *Parking in Town Centres*, Planning Bulletin No. 7, HMSO, 1965.

94

differently from most other commodities and that it is impossible and unnecessary to judge that one kind of parking is more important than another, or several short stays more efficient or important than one long stay.[1] Allocation is solely by price: prices that cover costs would supply the appropriate deterrent to the long-term parker and if a commercial vehicle or commercial premises cannot cover the costs of 'essential' or 'operational' parking this is an indication that they are making poor use of scarce space in its existing location. Further, although the administrative approach is sanctified by long usage, custom, and the pressure of various interests, and may in consequence be hard to change,[2] it must be remembered that parking charges are one of the few ways in which the costs of urban vehicle use can be brought home to the user

simply. Arbitrary restrictions are costly and difficult to enforce; partly because of 'low' charges (since raised) but also because of the costs of enforcement, costs absorbed 75 per cent of the revenue from London parking meters in 1963-64.[3]

An economic approach to parking could have substantial effects on parking and traffic. Off-street parking in city centres, whether multi-storey or underground, will presumably be the major provision when specialised road networks are created, and it is unlikely that it can be supplied at less than £1,000 per parking space at current prices.[4] To cover costs of this magnitude plus running costs, a revenue of at least £2 a week will be necessary per space, and, even assuming a high average utilisation rate of 40 hours per week, a charge of at least 1s. per hour will be necessary. The equilibrium

[1] G. J. Roth, *Paying for Parking*, Hobart Paper 33, IEA, 1965.

[2] On this it can be observed that people, not being taught the aims and effects of allocation of parking (and road space) by price, seem to prefer the allocation of these commodities by queuing, 'first come first served', administrative edict, congestion, and by other arbitrary or wasteful methods. Similarly local authorities, rejecting the full use of pricing as a determinant, have as a result to struggle to satisfy an apparently insatiable demand for parking.

[3] Ministry of Transport, *Report on Parking Meters, 1963-64*, HMSO, 1965.

[4] A. F. Holt, 'Comparative Costs of Car Parks', *The Surveyor*, 23 May, 1964.

price which equates supply and demand for on-street parking may well be higher. Charging these prices might have substantial effects in choking off parking demand and traffic, particularly long-term parkers and commuters.

On the quantitative aspects of parking demand three problems arise:

(1) How is parking space in residential areas to be provided? The long-term Buchanan principle—that the vehicle owner should be responsible for the parking of his vehicle off the carriageway—is sound and implies private provision of parking space. Although the suggestion will create little difficulty and cost in low density areas it will become an increasing problem in high density areas because it will require acquisition and demolition of houses; but, at the same time, it will supply appropriate incentives to re-develop 'twilight' areas, since difficulties in accommodating cars will increasingly affect the attractions and the market value of such housing (see Chapter 6).

(2) How are journeys or trips to be converted into parking demand at or near the town centre, with allowance for the peak accumulation of parked vehicles? For example 10,000 trips between 8 a.m. and 6 p.m. and an average duration of parking of two hours will result in an average parking demand for 2,000 vehicles in this period. If peak demand is 10 per cent above average, then a peak parking demand of 2,200 vehicles is attributable to the 10,000 trips. It may be noted that since peak parking demand tends to occur in mid-morning and mid-afternoon,[1] it may not be easy to control morning peak traffic by restricting total parking space. Flexible pricing as a method of control is therefore necessary.

(3) How is the cost of the peak accumulation of parking attracted by each central attractor to be 'debited' to him in planning? The difficulties in resolving this problem arise because no simple index such as floor space is capable of expressing the direct responsibility of a particular attractor for a given quantity of parking. Furthermore it is not easy to allocate parking to individual attractors when a trip has several destinations. Further planning research on this question seems to be required, although there seems little doubt that 'economic' charges for parking would resolve this question semi-automatically.

[1] Road Research Laboratory, *Research on Road Traffic*, HMSO, 1965.

CHAPTER 6

URBAN RENEWAL

ALTHOUGH THERE are many problems and opportunities in urban renewal—slum clearance, derelict sites, obsolete and badly sited industrial buildings—the most important arise in town centres and in the areas of 'twilight housing' erected before about 1921 and consequently in many ways below modern standards, though they may not be classified as slums.

Town centres

Commercial pressure for the renewal of town centres has encouraged an official attitude of partnership between the private developer and the planning authority, the developer using his capital and knowledge of the market in his proposals, the planning authority using its judgement and powers to guide plans into what it considers to be desirable directions.[1] In effect therefore, assuming conflict between commercial aims and 'good planning', the partnership results in a bargaining process between the developer seeking to maximise (within limits) his density of development and his profits, and the planning authority seeking to obtain the maximum amount of 'unremunerative' assets—roads, open spaces, parking, or the most 'desirable' overall lay-out—compatible with a level of profits that is just sufficient not to deter the developer from investing his capital.

Although this procedure may appear unexceptionable in principle and in accord with the procedure of development control somewhat expanded in scale, certain dangers and difficulties are likely to arise. Neither the developer (who ignores some of the costs of congestion)

[1] Ministries of Transport and Housing and Local Government, *Town Centres: Approach to Renewal*, Planning Bulletin No. 1, HMSO, 1962.

nor the planning authority with vague or unknown criteria are at present fully informed.

In the first place shopping and 'office' trends have been towards the continued growth of town centres in recent years; for example the growth of the multiple and the large retail unit at the expense of the smaller unit (see Chapter 7). But it has occurred in a period when urban transport was still dominated by public transport and this trend may be reversed when car ownership becomes more widespread and dominant. There is a danger then of over-provision of shopping space and of other 'attractors' in town centres, and of excessive centralisation; as we have indicated *decentralisation* may prove to be the correct answer to the urban traffic and planning conundrum. Though over-provision may be to some extent mitigated by the growth of population, *per capita* income and competition, it is necessary to analyse this more fully and we do so in Chapters 7 and 8.

In the second place, there is the problem of accommodating current schemes which are likely to be carried out in the next few years to long-term plans which have not yet been evolved. How serious this difficulty is likely to prove can only be seen in particular cases; *a priori* it may be or may not be a serious impediment to a sound long-term plan, but the risk that current schemes will reduce the opportunities for long-term development must exist.

Finally there is the danger that parking will take its habitual place and be regarded and planned as an unprofitable residual by the planning authority. This policy would weaken the power of the planning authority in the bargaining process with private developers. Also, particularly where restrictions are to be applied to traffic, parking should be charged at the full market value for central space; to restrict traffic and charge less than market prices for parking is to pursue mutually inconsistent policies.

RESIDENTIAL RENEWAL: THE CASE FOR INTERVENTION

Pressure for intervention by the public sector to encourage residential renewal or improvement is now strong. There were some 600,000 slums in 1960,[1] but apart from these there are 6.8 million

[1] M. F. W. Hemming, 'The Price of Accommodation,' NIESR *Economic Review*, August 1964.

other houses built before 1921[1] (about 40 per cent of the 1964 housing stock of 16.8 million in Great Britain) which cannot as yet be classified as slums and thus dealt with by health regulations and direct administrative action. Fundamentally the problem in 'twilight' areas is whether to subsidise the improvement of these houses and their environment, or to encourage demolition and comprehensive re-development.

Before considering residential renewal in detail it is necessary to explain why public intervention is required at all. There is after all a market for housing which supplies new housing to meet demand (both in the private and public sectors) and re-allocates existing housing. If for example a block of existing housing became obsolete and unattractive on a good site, re-development might be expected to be attractive and take place without intervention.

The case for intervention seems to arise fundamentally from the housing market and the various fiscal and legislative effects upon it.[2] In particular public policy has created two large privileged groups—the wealthier owner-occupier whose tax rebate on mortgage (and capital gains) increase with expenditure on housing, and the council tenant who is subsidised or favoured by charging historical costs rather than current market prices. The families excluded from these groups and thus from modern housing, either by income conditions imposed on mortgage repayments or by long waiting lists for council housing, are forced to concentrate their demands on older housing with low controlled or high market rents. Controlled tenants may be able to purchase these houses at bargain prices and though they in turn are often 'privileged', it is only by remaining in these older houses.[3]

Thus the lives of twilight houses have been artificially extended, a thesis which is confirmed by the combination of poor housing with a low average proportion of income spent on housing in Britain (9 per cent) which reaches its peak (or zenith) in Scotland

---

[1] P. A. Stone, 'Urban Standards and National Resources', *Town Planning Review*, October 1965.

[2] A. J. Merrett and A. Sykes, *Housing Finance and Development*, Longmans Green, 1965.

[3] The disadvantages of house-directed as opposed to family-directed aid are discussed on p. 111.

where the combination of low subsidised rents and poor housing is widespread.

The size of these favoured groups makes it politically difficult to rectify the distortions and there may therefore be a case for intervening to ameliorate their effects. The disadvantages of trying to remedy one distortion by another are obvious and many economists have argued that the solution must be to go to the root of the problem by abolishing the original distortions.[1] Thus the resources released by more discrimination in housing subsidies might be devoted to urban renewal.

Intervention to promote urban renewal has sometimes been called for because of the unwillingness of owners to improve their property unless neighbouring owners do the same, or the difficulties of assembling sites arising from individual rights in property. But these situations do not seem to justify intervention but rather gradual acquisition as properties fall vacant or are sold. However the valid reasons seem to be:

(1)   To rectify the distortions outlined above so long as they are not removed, i.e. to improve the housing of the poorer families excluded from the two privileged groups.

(2)   To prevent a sequence whereby housing demand is met largely by new building on new sites, whilst 'twilight' housing and its sites remain under-utilised and undeveloped, and increasingly decay.

The rationale behind urban renewal policies seems therefore grounded in the distortions imposed by public policy on the housing market. Specific assistance to the needy who are badly housed would also be justified even if current distortions in the housing market were removed, but caution is necessary.

Some of the occupants of 'twilight' housing would probably prefer their present housing at low rents or prices to better housing at higher rents and prices and would neither welcome, nor be able to accept, better housing forced upon them directly (on site) or indirectly by re-location elsewhere. It might be considered right in these cases to subordinate the rights, demands and preferences of the individual to those of the majority, for example by compulsory purchase and re-development, but it would be a hard case to prove.

[1] For instance John Carmichael, *Vacant Possession*, Hobart Paper 28, IEA, 1964.

It is therefore important that the reasons for the inadequacies of the housing market should be clearly established and means to encourage urban renewal tailored accordingly: for urban renewal measures must also be reconciled with the wider logic required in housing policy. In the USA[1] urban renewal has often worsened the lot of the least fortunate families. With this experience in mind it is as well to remind ourselves that the aim of residential renewal is not simply to improve the physical fabric of our cities, *but to increase total welfare in so doing*. Improving the lot of the more fortunate families at the expense of the least fortunate is hardly likely to do this.

New houses—building for residential renewal
In the above it has been argued that the case for intervention in residential renewal arises essentially from the distortions of the housing market, and that intervention should ideally take the form of aiding the least fortunate families. It is still true however that new housing supplied to the general market, over and above that required to meet population growth, will to some extent enable existing houses to 'filter down' the housing market to these families. There is a case then for looking at future housing output globally in the conventional forecasting way to see the implications for residential renewal, although the dangers of doing this, and the reservations above, must be borne in mind.

Initially the familiar problems arise of how far we would like to look ahead and how far in practice we can. In choosing a 40-year planning period one is not only aiming at consistency with a possible long-term traffic plan but also trying to allow for the durability of housing and the long period required to accumulate sufficient investment to change our housing stock substantially. Because of the uncertainties and difficulties of prediction over such a long period only broad orders of magnitude and broad alternatives can be very tentatively considered. It is also as well to remind ourselves at this point that if the efficiency of the relevant markets are improved, particularly those for roads and housing, we can reduce our reliance upon long-term plans and forecasts. Since

[1] 'America's Cities', *The Economist*, 6 February, 1965; Martin Anderson *The Federal Bulldozer*, Massachusetts Institute of Technology Press, 1965.

these markets are currently very imperfect we must accept *pro tem* that central assessment of future possibilities is inevitable.

Because of the varying incidence of 'twilight' housing, some towns, particularly in the north, consist almost entirely of pre-1921 housing. One must therefore approach residential renewal as a national rather than purely local or individual problem: assistance from the relatively more to the relatively less favoured regions is implied.

This 'twilight' housing consists mainly of two-storey buildings at densities of 20 to 30 to the acre and it is therefore unlikely to be considered or made satisfactory in the future if standards of living continue to increase. We shall therefore discuss the renewal problem initially in terms of new housing and look forward to the eventual replacement of virtually all 'twilight' housing. Such a programme offers maximum scope for the advantages of comprehensive redevelopment plans. We shall estimate how much the economy and individual families will be able and willing to devote to new housing in the future and consider the implications of these estimates for urban renewal by the progressive demolition of 'twilight' housing and the construction of new.

For new housing the obvious starting point is the current housing target of 500,000 houses per annum (UK) which the National Plan aims to achieve in 1970; the per capita share for Great Britain is 485,000. This target may be regarded as the minimum programme for the rest of the century in view of the growth in population and other pressures for urban renewal. Perhaps a more realistic estimate of future house-building would be the 485,000 target (in 1970) as a base, rising at an annual rate of 2 per cent. At a growth rate of 3 per cent per annum in GNP (Chapter 5), a 2 per cent annual rate of increase in new housing could be obtained with a 1 per cent annual rate of increase in the size or quality of new houses without increasing the share of national resources devoted to new housing, provided that productivity in new housing increased at the average rate for the economy as a whole. With the spread of industrial building and more planning of traditional building operations, this target should be possible, and an annual rate of increase in the output of new housing of 2 per cent is therefore modest and realistic. The price of houses (including land) will probably rise in relation to the prices of other goods and services because of the increasing impact of a higher population on planning controls, but the rise in land prices should not absorb any of the economy's current resources.

Communal and individual ability to pay for housing
Although the economy should be able to supply 485,000 new houses *per annum* with a diminishing proportion of its total output (after 1970) and a constant proportion of its output in the case of the 2 per cent per annum rate of increase, it may be objected that households would not be willing to spend such a large proportion of their income on new housing.

At the root of this argument is the relatively low proportion of income currently spent on housing in the UK and the fact that expenditure on it does not increase at the same rate as income, as the Ministry of Labour expenditure surveys have shown. However the housing market is so distorted by rent controls, security of tenure and other difficulties in changing houses, and conventional or haphazard rents for council houses, that expenditure data gives little indication of what families would freely choose to spend on housing in a free market.

The most reliable data on this subject is that relating to expenditure by owner-occupiers at present buying their houses which suggest that families' expenditure on housing would increase at about the same rate as income, but even this may be an understatement. Another factor favouring new housing in the future will be the rising real cost of repairs. The lack of scope for mechanisation of repair work makes it unlikely that productivity per head will increase at the same rate as in the rest of the economy; rising real wage-rates will thus cause the real costs of repairs to rise and may lead to increasing substitution of new housing for old and 'do-it-yourself' as opposed to hired professional repairs (at least among owner-occupiers).

It is now possible to discuss the effect of the minimum target of 485,000 houses per annum by the end of the century, and the modest maximum alternative programme of 485,000 houses in 1970, increasing at 2 per cent per annum until the end of the century, which would result in an output of about 1 million houses in the year 2004. In 1964 there were some 16.8 million houses and households in Great Britain: the 'shortage' of dwellings in London was compensated almost exactly by a surplus elsewhere.[1] The provision of new housing, before it can begin to replace the existing housing stock, must cover several elements of demand:

(i) *Provision for future growth in population.* The population of Great Britain is currently forecast by the Registrar-General to increase from about 52 million in 1964 to 72 million in 2004 on the assumption that birth rates remain as at present,[2] requiring an estimated 7 million dwellings to cover this growth. If however marriage and birth rates rise in accordance with the 1931-1961 experience, the population in 2004 can be expected to be 85 million which would require an additional 9.2 million dwellings. But if marriage and fertility rates gradually decline to the 1940 level, population can be expected to rise to only 65 million by 2004, requiring an extra 6.3 million dwellings.[3] These estimates will be regarded as maxima and minima.

(ii) *Provision of dwellings to relieve the current shortage which exists principally in London, and to create a surplus in order to encourage mobility.* This figure may be put at 650,000 dwellings or about $2\frac{1}{2}$ per cent of the expected housing stock by the end of the century.

(iii) *Houses for families willing and able to acquire a second house* (new or old). It is difficult to estimate this figure but increasing real incomes may raise it to as much as $2\frac{1}{2}$ million dwellings, or about 10 per cent of the expected number of families by the end of the century.

A NATIONAL PROGRAMME FOR RESIDENTIAL RENEWAL

In working out a national programme for residential renewal two preliminary assumptions must be made: (i) that there is a national pool of housing so that any growth in the stock of housing, over and above that necessary to cover growth in population, can be applied in effect to replacement of the worst housing in Great

---

[1] M. F. W. Hemming, *op. cit.*

[2] Such assumptions, though necessary for forecasting, are very far from invulnerable. In 1956, for example, the Registrar General's population forecast for the year 1996 was 46 million (England and Wales). By 1963 the forecast for the year 2003 had been revised upwards to 64 million. This major adjustment was necessary because of an unexpected increase in the birth rate.

[3] P. A. Stone, *op. cit.*

TABLE VII
Maximum and Minimum Housing Targets for Great Britain,
1965–2004
Millions

Target	Output of new housing	Demand for new housing	New housing in replacement	Oldest remaining house in 2004 built in year	Age of oldest house in 2004
I. 0·485 million new houses *per annum*	18·6	9·45[1]	9·15	1931	73
II. 0·485 million new houses plus 2% increase *per annum*	26·35	12·35[2]	14·0	1956	48

[1] Consisting of 6.3 million dwellings to accommodate population growth to 65 million plus 0.65 million 'surplus' houses and 2.5 million second houses.

[2] Consisting of 9.2 million houses to accommodate population growth to 85 million plus 0.65 million surplus houses and 2.5 million second houses.

Britain (problems arising from the geographical distribution of poor quality housing are initially ignored); and (ii) that age of housing is an index of poor quality. This assumption is necessary for want of any other simple guide to condition and ability to meet households' demands though in some cases it is absurd; many old houses have charm and character, are in good condition and command high prices. But in relation to total housing stock the numbers of such houses are very small: the Housing Survey[1] shows that less than 10 per cent of the housing stock was erected before 1861, and only a fraction of this number, perhaps 10 per cent, seems likely to fall into this category, that is, 1 per cent of the total, or some 170,000 *homes*. About 81,000 *buildings* of historic or architectural interest were listed in 1961.[2] These assumptions, particularly that of a national 'pool' of housing, will be re-examined later in this Chapter.

Table VII estimates the implications for urban renewal in Great Britain of the minimum target of 485,000 new houses a year

[1] Central Office of Information, *The Housing Situation in 1960*, HMSO, 1962.
[2] Central Office of Information, *Town Planning in Britain*, HMSO, 1962.

and the minimum expected population increase and similarly for the maximum target of 485,000 houses plus 2 per cent annual rate of increase and the maximum expected population increase. Minimum housing output is married to minimum future population (and maximum to maximum) because the size of future population increase will of course affect both the output of the economy (including housing) and demand for housing.

Table VII shows that, *on the assumptions made*, the *minimum* estimates of housing output and population would allow the replacement of all dwellings erected before 1931 giving the age of the oldest house remaining as 73 years in 2004 (line I), or that the *maximum* housing target and population estimate would allow the replacement of all houses erected before 1956 giving the age of the oldest dwelling remaining as 48 years in 2004 (line II). For both programmes, insofar as families acquired older houses as second houses (pre-1956 or pre-1931 for both programmes respectively), the replacement of older unwanted housing could proceed further. If for example all second houses acquired were pre-1956, all other unwanted houses built before 1964 could be replaced in the maximum programme, and if all second houses were pre-1931, all other unwanted houses built before 1938 could be replaced. But, since demand for second houses will presumably be for country houses or cottages in attractive areas, or perhaps for town flats, the scope for meeting this demand by the retention and improvement of older houses would be limited by their numbers and location. The maximum programme may be extravagant in the sense that population increase will not be as large as that assumed and families might not in practice choose such a high rate of replacement. But the target would be within our technical and economic abilities if a 3 per cent growth rate could be achieved, and it is perhaps a more realistic programme than the 485,000 a year output. In any case it should be possible to replace as a national minimum all pre-1931 housing and as a national maximum all pre-1956 housing by the end of the century.

Obstacles to the programme
There are several obstacles to the realisation of these programmes, a first being that the ideal of a national pool of housing cannot in practice be achieved and that building resources and urban

renewal 'needs' would not, as we have assumed, have the same geographical distribution. In particular building resources will be concentrated where population growth and demand are highest and the switch to a growth *and* replacement market indicated in Table VII would require a shift in the geographical distribution of building, in particular from the South to the North. It would almost certainly necessitate a higher proportion of new housing to be provided by the public sector and also undesirable and awkward controls on building if private demand stays buoyant and threatens to exceed house-building capacity.

Rather than change the geographical distribution of new building to conform with existing renewal needs, something of the same effect could be obtained by migration from areas of older housing to areas of newer housing, or by housing migrants in new housing elsewhere; the net effect of these measures would tend to be vacation of the worst housing. To some extent movement of residents may of course be desirable as in the cases of migration to new towns, growth points or local over-spill schemes. But long distance migration from older to newer housing areas, say from North to South, may be undesirable and the provision of new housing on the scale envisaged in Table VII demands at least *some* direct replacement on existing sites, if urban areas are not to spread indefinitely while twilight areas decay.

In spite of the difficulties of altering the geographical distribution of new building so that it coincides with population growth *and* urban renewal 'needs', it should be an attainable minimum objective to replace (if so desired and if quality warrants) all pre-1921 housing by the end of the century in all areas. As an aid to long-term planning, every authority should be able to draw up a building programme covering estimated population growth (or decline) plus urban renewal 'needs', thus indicating the planning opportunities and problems.

The siting of new housing to replace existing houses
Apart from problems of making the broad distribution of building output coincide with geographical distribution of population growth and urban renewal 'needs', there is the further more local difficulty of the siting of new housing so as to replace existing marginal housing. This problem arises from the market prices of

'twilight' housing; although government intervention is implied in urban renewal, acquisition and compensation must be at market prices (both in law and in order to secure economically sound policies). Broadly speaking it appears at the present time (1966) that the market prices of the majority of pre-1921 housing is within the £500—£1,500 range, more of course in fashionable or overcrowded areas. At densities of 20 to 30 houses to the acre, the costs of these sites is between £10,000 and £45,000 per acre plus costs of clearance, which is substantially above prices for most virgin sites under existing planning policies. With site costs at these levels there are two main alternatives for housing—high density re-development in the form of flats to minimise the impact of site costs per dwelling,[1] or lower density development on cheaper virgin land at the outskirts.

High development may be appropriate near town centres but this form of building is costly and counter to the preferences of most families (Chapter 7). Taking into account such difficulties as accommodating vehicles, this solution may be inappropriate. The alternative of new building on virgin land on the outskirts may also be undesirable, because, although new building and increasing decay may ultimately bring down the market price of 'twilight' housing and make its redevelopment profitable, the net result may be more urban spread[2] than if a more direct attack on existing housing had been made. The prospect of about 20 million new houses by 2004 mainly on virgin sites is not obviously attractive in planning terms, and purely to avoid this consequence some subsidy to residential renewal may be justified.

At present the best policy for re-development of 'twilight' housing seems to be: (i) some spread or decentralisation of central activities to nearby areas of re-development; (ii) some of the space to be occupied by new roads and other ancillaries such as car parks and multi-level intersections; (iii) re-development at density appropriate to land values, building costs, families' preferences and distance from centre (Chapter 7); (iv) some overspill population

---

[1] *Urban Renewal: Fulham Study*, Taylor Woodrow Group, 1963.

[2] General under-occupation of the existing housing stock, arising from controls and low rents for families remaining in their existing houses, would also encourage this tendency.

to be housed at lower density at the perimeter or dispersed to new or expanded towns.

Ownership of twilight housing

A final obstacle to residential renewal, particularly among pre-1914 houses, lies in the problem of ownership. Before 1914, when rent control was introduced as a temporary war-time expedient, houses were erected by private landlords for rent, but now ownership falls broadly into two classes:

(i) Property owned by private landlords, often of slender means, and let at low rents (controlled and uncontrolled). Because of the past history of rent control, these landlords in general have little remaining interest in improving their property (see below) but would probably be favourable to acquisition and re-development at market prices for vacant possession. Private landlords owned about 52 per cent of pre-1921 housing in 1960 in England and Wales.

(ii) Property owned by owner-occupiers, who have acquired it from private landlords, often at low prices during controlled tenancies and rents when housing was unprofitable to private landlords. In general, because of their personal stake in their homes, owner-occupiers are likely to favour improvement to their property (see below). About 44 per cent of pre-1921 housing in England and Wales was owner-occupied in 1960.[1]

On the whole, then, owner-occupation of 'twilight' housing favours improvement (although improvement grants are not taken up on a substantial scale) and opposition to acquisition and re-development. Private landlords, on the other hand, tend to favour acquisition and re-development, though the tenants' interests may oppose it. Also since ownership by private landlords and owner-occupiers is about equal, there would if reproduced in sites or blocks —the relevant unit for re-development—be difficulties in carrying out renewal.

Two approaches to acquisition and re-development are possible— acquisition by compulsory purchase order against possibly serious opposition, or the gradual accumulation of properties by the housing authority when properties are vacated by existing owners and

---

[1] The remaining 4 per cent of pre-1914 housing was owned by local authorities. (*The Housing Situation in 1960, op. cit.*)

tenants. The second process is better because 'twilight' housing may be predominantly occupied by elderly people (as a result of rent control and immobility), a fact that suggests gradual acquisition and eventual renewal.

Improvement of 'twilight' housing that cannot soon be replaced

In addition to an eventual replacement programme, a policy for encouraging the repair and re-equipment of pre-1914 housing which cannot soon be replaced, and for improving its external environment, would probably be worthwhile as assistance to the poorly housed, even though the remaining lives of these properties will be limited.

For the future must be discounted quite heavily by the rate of interest when considering the present value of a given investment or improvement so that a disproportionate part of the benefits from an improvement occurs in the earlier years of its life. If we take an improvement to a house with a remaining life of 40 years as standard, at a rate of interest of 7 per cent, 95 per cent of the present value of future benefits will arise in the first 30 years of its remaining life, 80 per cent in the first 20 years of remaining life, and 55 per cent in the first 10 years of remaining life.

In addition to the welfare case for improving houses with a limited life, there is a more practical case for concentrating on improvements with an appropriately short remaining life (e.g. by re-painting). Here the aim is to ensure that the investment in improvement yields up its full value over the remaining life of the house and to avoid both excessive investment and adding substantially to future market prices, so making eventual acquisition and redevelopment more difficult.

Any effort to encourage improvement of the fabric and equipment of aged housing will be difficult unless the extreme of compulsory powers available under the 1964 Housing Act are used.[1] With some millions of houses eligible, only 37,500 general improvement grants were made in 1963, and only 77,000 standard amenities grants;[2] although owner-occupiers owned a smaller proportion

---

[1] M. F. W. Hemming, *op. cit.*

[2] That is, grants for the provision of one or all of the following, bath or shower, wash hand-basin, W.C., hot water supply and food store.

of pre-1921 housing in 1960, they took up some 2½ times the number
of grants made to private landlords.[1]

Since grants and improvements seem unlikely to be taken up on
a large scale, the part that can be played by repair in a programme
of residential improvement will probably be small. In the long run
it is therefore inevitable that a large proportion of 'twilight' housing
will deteriorate—the primary justification of a policy of eventual
replacement.

Conclusions

Town centre renewal schemes, which will vary in detail, carry the
danger of increased concentration on the town centre and aggrava-
tion of urban congestion. Pre-1921 housing will be basically unsuited
to people's demands in the future, because of rising real costs of
repairs and the reluctance of owners to undertake improvements.
It therefore seems clear that the future of existing 'twilight' housing
must eventually lie mainly in re-development. But because of
the barriers to distributing new building in accordance with
population growth and renewal 'needs' and the difficulties of ownership and acquisition, redevelopment will not be easy. Residential
renewal may in that event take the form of new housing on virgin
sites, thus increasing urban spread.

Nevertheless it should be possible as a minimum to replace (if so
desired) all pre-1921 housing in England and Wales by the end of
the century and local authorities should be able to draw up renewal
and improvement programmes as an aid to planning. Any residential
renewal programmes and measures to achieve them must be
reconciled with general housing problems and the wider logic
required in housing policy. There is little doubt that distortions of
the housing market by rent control, subsidies, house-directed
rather than family-directed aid, and the consequent frustration of the
allocative function of the price mechanism, have aggravated housing
shortages and perpetuated the lives of 'twilight' housing. Intervention
therefore should preferably be by gradual acquisition of 'twilight'
properties and eventual re-development, with compulsory purchase
only as a last resort, for there are considerable dangers of worsening
the lot of the least fortunate families.

[1] M. F. W. Hemming, op. cit.

CHAPTER 7

DENSITY AND DISTRIBUTION OF THE POPULATION

THE DEMAND FOR ACCOMMODATION

THE DOMINANT theme in urban renewal and town traffic problems is how far we should maintain our towns and cities broadly in their present form and densities, with planning controls and long-term restrictions on traffic, or how far should major centres of population and economic activity be encouraged to disperse at lower densities with more freedom for traffic but some net loss of open countryside. As a last resort, further spread of large existing urban areas at lower densities, although probably the least satisfactory alternative, may need to be considered. Whichever policy is chosen and to whatever degree it is enforced, the forecast increase in population of perhaps 40 per cent by the end of the century will need to be accommodated.

In discussing densities and population distribution it is important to avoid dogmatism and abstraction and to concentrate on analysis of the main issues. These are on the one hand the demands and preferences of families for living, travel and amenities and on the other the technical and economic forces determining the distribution of economic activity.

Preferences for living space and gardens
The most important choice for the family is that between a house and a flat and its preference will have a fundamental effect on the density and distribution of population in terms of living space. Houses with gardens provide safe and convenient areas for children's play, family recreation, hobbies and car-parking facilities together

with more freedom to make and avoid noise. All these amenities can be provided in flats but only at additional cost. Compared with houses, however, flats offer more opportunities for social contact and for communal living which, depending on the inhabitants' personalities, homogeneity and sense of common background, may be valued by them positively or negatively.

In surveys of families' preferences as between a house and a flat, most of the evidence is that the majority would prefer a house. Thus Dr P. A. Stone[1] reports that 'it would appear from opinion surveys and the reports of housing managers that not more than 20 per cent of families would find a flat a fully acceptable alternative to a house', and Professor Peter Self[2] states that successive social surveys have shown that 'anything from 80 to 90 per cent of the working population will plump for the house if the rents are the same'.

Other evidence is relevant in indicating families' choices between high- and low-density living. In *Gardening Survey* (carried out and published by Contimart[3] in April 1964) it is shown that 80 per cent of households in Britain had gardens, the South-West and Wales being highest at 87 per cent, the North-West lowest at 58 per cent. These percentages may be misleading because to some extent they reflect *past* preferences, the historical development of housing and families' adaptation to the existing housing stock rather than families' *current* preferences. Of more relevance, therefore, particularly in a society expected to become increasingly wealthy, is the ownership of gardens by income group or social class. 68 per cent of DEs, the lowest social group, had gardens in Britain and 91 per cent of ABs. Again, 59 per cent of DEs had gardens of less than 2,500 sq. ft. but only 23 per cent of ABs. For those larger than 2,500 sq.ft., the percentage was consistently higher for ABs than for DEs. 15 per cent of ABs had gardens of 2,500—5,000 sq.ft. compared with 10 per cent of DEs; 13 per cent of ABs possessed gardens of over ½-acre (about 23,000 sq.ft.) compared with only 2 per cent of DEs. There seems little doubt then that the demand for more spacious living tends to grow with income and social class.

[1] P. A. Stone, *Housing, Town Development, Land and Costs*, Estates Gazette, 1963.
[2] P. Self, *Cities in Flood*, Faber, 1958.
[3] Contimart Ltd., *Gardening Survey*, Contimart, 1964.

The choice between work and leisure

In addition to expected changes in income per head there is the possibility of reductions in working hours and an increase in leisure time. A good deal has been written and said about the effects of automation, reduction of working hours to absorb redundancy, and the spectacular increase in leisure that will result. But the evidence does not suggest that there will be spectacular reductions in working hours and increases in leisure in Britain. Between 1952 and 1963 when gross national product per head (at constant prices) increased by about 25 per cent, average weekly hours worked in manufacturing fell by only 2.5 per cent although they fluctuated with the level of economic activity.[1] An analysis of working hours in Western Europe by the *Financial Times* in 1961 indicated that the average hours worked in all countries differed little from 2,000 a year, though there were wide variations in working habits, paid and public holidays. It seems unlikely therefore on present evidence, which is admittedly not very conclusive, that average working hours will decline by more than about a third by the end of the century, that is from about 47 hours in 1963 to about 32 hours.

The immediate effect of reduction in working hours will be that the working population, which is about half the total population, will have increased leisure, although the increase will not be large.[2] The effect on preferences for living space will depend of course on how it is spent. Recent trends in Britain suggest a large increase in outdoor semi-rural activities, but such is the climate that some of the increased leisure time will be spent at home, and hence may increase preferences for houses with gardens rather than for flats, if only to accommodate cars, boats and other home-based leisure goods and activities.

Perhaps the most decisive change that would follow an increase in leisure would be a change from the five- to four-day working week. Just as a general change from a six- day to a five-day week during the 1950s encouraged families to decentralise to pleasant rural surroundings and travel longer distances to work, so a transition

[1] NIESR *Economic Review*, Statistical Appendix, August 1964.
[2] Allowing for eight hours' sleep and one hour per day for travel to work, etc., a reduction in the working week from 47 to 32 hours will increase disposable leisure time per week from 60 to 75 hours a week, an increase of 25 per cent, but only for workers.

from the five- to the four-day working week can be expected to extend the trend. Having moved to more rural, spacious surroundings, families would be unlikely voluntarily to choose denser forms of living in flats. Thus the transition to a four-day working week will be likely to reinforce the already rising demand for decentralised living in houses with gardens rather than flats.

The evidence for low density is strong but it cannot be regarded as entirely conclusive. In the first place, the replies given to hypothetical questions may not reflect people's behaviour when given a choice, and secondly, flats are much rarer than houses so that replies may be biased by a conventional picture of an ideal house. Finally, more than 50 per cent of British families are without children; the disadvantages of flats for these families are probably less and their advantages correspondingly more.

It is possible therefore that, given more individual mobility between dwellings, families, at least before children are born and after they leave home, would prefer a flat. A higher proportion of the population (perhaps up to one-half) could therefore be housed in flats and still have their dwelling preferences met over time.

Comparative costs of houses and flats
The general preference of British families seems to be for a house with a garden rather than a flat. Nevertheless the relative costs of houses and flats must be considered before policy decisions can be made; if houses cost substantially more than flats, families' preferences may not be sufficiently strong to be decisive. The evidence in recent years however has been that the building costs of flats are substantially above those of houses of similar size, though the differences may be reduced in future if industrialised building is adopted on any scale.

To analyse the building costs of flats compared with houses, we must rely mainly on the well-known work of Dr Stone, which has been broadly confirmed by more recent cost estimates published by the Ministry of Housing and Local Government.[1] Dr Stone analysed the average relative building costs for blocks of flats and maisonettes of different heights with the results shown in Table VIII.

[1] *Housing Cost Yardstick*, Design Bulletin No. 7, HMSO, 1963.

TABLE VIII

Relative Average Prices Per Dwelling for Blocks of Flats and Maisonettes

Storey Height	Inner London	Outer London	Provinces	Outer London Smoothed Curve
2	100	100	100	100
3	130	127	124	120
4	136	137	133	136
5	142	—	148	148
6	135	158	180	157
7	148	173	197	164
8	141	165	187	170
9	148	173	196	175
10	144	168	192	179
11	158	185	210	182
12	158	185	210	185

Source: P. A. Stone, *Housing, Town Development, Land and Costs,* Estates Gazette, 1963.

With costs for 2-storey development as 100 in all cases, the differences between the rate at which costs rise per storey in London (inner and outer) and the provinces need to be noted: low blocks of 3-storeys are relatively more costly in London, whereas the costs of high blocks in the provinces rise more steeply. Dr Stone attributes the latter difference to the larger volume and experience of high building in London, and as experience of building high spreads he considers that the smoothed curve for outer London would be the most representative. From this curve the increase in average cost per storey added varies from 20 per cent between 2 and 3 storeys to only 3 per cent between 11 and 12 storeys.

The implications for housing and planning policies of these costs are brought out by calculations made by Dr Stone.[1] For any given set of dwelling costs and land prices there is a corresponding block height for which total initial costs per dwelling (excluding maintenance, etc.) are at a minimum. At 1957 costs for building (of 3-bedroom provincial dwellings), clearance, roads, and public utilities, Dr Stone has calculated the land price that would minimise

[1] P. A. Stone, *op. cit.*

TABLE IX

Number of Storeys and Land Prices Giving Minimum Average Initial Costs

No. of storeys	Density in dwellings per acre	Price of land per acre £
2	20	—
3	26	24,000
4	31	29,000
5	35	32,000
6	38	35,000
7	40	37,000
8	41	40,000
9	42	42,000
10	43	44,000
12	44	46,000

Source: Stone, *op. cit.*

the total initial costs[1] per dwelling at various heights of buildings, i.e. the price of land that would justify construction of 2, 3, 4, etc., storeys (Table IX).

The figures in Table IX suggest that a land price of £24,000 an acre would justify construction of 3-storey blocks, a land price of £29,000 an acre would justify 4-storey blocks, and so on, at 1957 initial costs. Curiously enough, it may be noted that the optimum density in dwellings per acre to minimise average total costs per dwelling corresponds closely with the price of land in thousands of £ per acre. For example a land price of £24,000 per acre would justify *up to* 26 dwellings to the acre, whilst a land price of £46,000 would justify *up to* 44 dwellings to the acre.[2] It should be noted that the land price that would justify construction of blocks of various

[1] It was argued in Chapter 2 that land values are not a cost to the economy as a whole: they are a measure of the advantages of access to land. The calculations of Table IX can thus be regarded as a balance between rising building costs with height, and the advantages of access.

[2] Lest anyone should be tempted to make a 'standard' or formula out of this proposition, it must be emphasised that it is only the density which minimises average total costs (land plus building) per dwelling. Insofar as families would be willing to pay more for additional space (or lower density) the optimum density will be lower, and the standard, if such can be set, will be a maximum one.

TABLE X

Capital Cost to the Community per Acre of Land Saved by Building High Flats Instead of Two-Storey Flats

No. of storeys	Capital Cost per Acre of Land Saved £000's
3	26·0
4	30·4
5	45·8
6	46·4
7	48·8
8	50·8
9	52·6
10	53·8
12	56·4

Source: Stone, *op. cit.*

---

heights will vary directly with building costs, so that for 1966 price levels these land prices must be increased by some 20 per cent.

Since land values are not independently determined but also depend on planning policies, to avoid circularity in reasoning, perhaps the most meaningful way in which the above building cost data can be presented is to regard the costs of higher density development as the price paid to save land. This calculation has been made by Dr Stone and is given in Table X.

Allowing for the increase in building costs since 1957, the marginal cost of saving land varies from about £31,000 an acre when 3-storey flats are built, to about £67,000 an acre when 12-storey flats are built. Only with extreme pressures, problems and policies such as occur in London and in other conurbations, or on valuable and accessible central sites, could such additional costs to save land be justified.

One particular influence favourable to dense development not taken into account is the saving in transport costs achievable by dense compared with spacious development. In practice of course there is no necessary relationship between the density of a given development and the inhabitants' transport costs, but in principle it is clear that compact development and shorter distances between origins and destinations should secure savings in the inhabitants' transport costs.

To take an example of 1,000 families to be housed at various densities, let us assume that they will form a completely self-contained community in which all wants (employment, shopping, schools, etc.) are met internally at the centre of a circular settlement of uniform density and building height. Then if the gross residential density is (say) 10 dwellings per acre, the area of the settlement will be 100 acres, and the radius will be about 400 yards. It can be shown that the average distance to the centre for all families will be 2/3rds of the radius so that if each family has 3.0 persons and each person makes one trip to centre each day, total person mileage per annum will be about 330,000. If personal transport costs, objective and subjective (the time and discomfort associated with walking), are valued at, say, 3d. per person-mile, the annual transport costs may be put at about £4,000 per annum. Capitalised at the reciprocal of the rate of interest (assumed to be 5 per cent) to make costs comparable with those in Tables IX and X, transport costs may be regarded as equivalent to a capital cost of £80,000 for the 10-dwellings per acre development. This 'capital cost of transport' would fall to about £56,000 for a density of 20 dwellings to the acre, a saving of £24,000 or £24 per dwelling, and would reduce still further for development at 40 dwellings to the acre. For this density the capital cost of transport would be £40,000, a further saving of £16,000 or £16 per dwelling. Therefore, although the savings in transport costs obtainable in principle from more compact development and higher densities are relevant, they are not sufficiently large to affect substantially any conclusions on densities.

It may be concluded therefore both on families' preferences and on the building cost side, the evidence still seems to be in favour of spacious development at low densities except where preferences and circumstances involve housing on valuable central sites. Families' preferences may of course change, particularly if, with increasing ability and desire to change dwellings, they should elect to live in flats for a higher proportion of their lives. This conclusion would then have to be modified. Similarly, if future changes in building techniques and costs, in particular industrialised building, should bring down the *relative* costs of high blocks, the case for higher densities would be strengthened.

THE DISTRIBUTION OF ECONOMIC ACTIVITY

In considering the distribution of economic activities which can independently sustain the prosperity of an area it must be emphasised that, although only 50 per cent of total population is working, this factor will tend to be the dominant one and will broadly determine the distribution of the entire population. It is true of course that the retired can divorce themselves almost entirely from centres of work and be relatively free to choose their location and distribution. Also, if workers travel longer distances to work a somewhat different distribution of population from that determined by the distribution of economic activity may emerge. There are obvious limits in these cases, and the extent to which the existing concentrations of activity will decentralise or be encouraged to do so, is crucial to the question of decentralisation of the population.

Economic activity is conventionally divided into manufacturing and service industries, although the latter can be regarded as independent in only a limited sense. Current trends and our ability to influence them differ for the two classes of industry.

(1) *Manufacturing*

In manufacturing, the growth in employment between 1952 and 1962 has been comparatively modest, only 6½ per cent as compared with an overall growth in employment in England and Wales of 10 per cent (Chapter 1). There is little doubt that the ability to encourage a different distribution of industrial expansion from that which would be determined by the market, by the industrial development certificate procedure and other positive inducements, has been moderately successful and applied firmly. The ability to build or extend a factory of less than 5,000 sq. ft. appears a possible loop-hole in control of industrial development, but it is doubtful if many units of less than 5,000 sq. ft. are sufficiently large to be independent and potentially mobile, and therefore able to select their own location. The only substantial loop-hole then arises from factories gradually extending in many units of, say, 4,999 sq. ft[1] and even this one is to be virtually closed by the proposals of the Control of Office and Industrial Development Act.[2]

[1] D. L. Foley, *Controlling London's Growth*, University of California Press, 1963.

[2] Control of Offices and Industrial Development Act, HMSO, 1964.

Economics and operations are favourable to decentralisation for a wide range of manufacturing industry, either to the outskirts of large urban centres or to more distant locations. Being an extensive rather than an intensive user of land (particularly in modern mass-production processes) manufacturing industry tends to be displaced from city centres by more intensive and profitable uses of urban land such as shops and offices, although inertia and the slow pace of change mean that uses that are uneconomic in the long term may linger on in inappropriate locations. The goods transport problems of industry are also eased by peripheral rather than central locations and, if one firm has close linkages with other firms and markets, they tend to take the form of transfers of goods (raw materials, intermediate products, and finished goods) which can be transported longer distances with little effect on firms' total costs, rather than the personal contacts which are important in the service industries.

In practice the major difficulty in encouraging the decentralisation of industry towards new locations arises in recruiting skilled people. They may not be available locally in sufficient numbers, and it may be difficult to attract suitable people from larger centres if the range of amenities is smaller and the choice of jobs is more restricted.

Although the distribution of manufacturing industry is more easily controlled and it has more incentive to decentralise than service industries, the rate of increase in employment in manufacturing industry is comparatively low. In any event controls are applicable only to physical expansion of premises and cannot be applied to existing premises and employment without heavy compensation.

Industrial location can be most easily influenced when industry is expanding and the expansions can be hived off into independent potentially mobile units; but in practice there is little mobile manufacturing industry to influence and existing concentrations can for the most part only be dispersed voluntarily over a long period. However some physical expansion of premises may still need to take place even though employment may be static or declining, particularly where bulky capital equipment and processes are substituted for labour. But if employment is not expanding there will be a smaller incentive on the part of the industrialist to move away from congested areas of labour shortage, and less reason to refuse an industrial development certificate when physical expansion does not entail an increase in employment.

(2)   Service industries

When we consider those service industries that can independently sustain the prosperity of an area—'offices' as they are commonly and rather vaguely called—the situation is different. As shown in Chapter 2, employment in these industries (e.g. professional and scientific services, insurance, banking and finance) increased by as much as 30 to 40 per cent between 1952 and 1962, and there is little doubt that this is the net result of technical advance and the substitution of capital for labour in manufacturing industry or agriculture, the maintenance of full employment and a high general level of demand, and the absorption of manpower into service industries for which demand expands. Furthermore the locational pull of offices to the central area of towns and cities is undoubtedly strong. Although there seems no tendency for offices to concentrate in the larger towns and cities, at least in 1951, as C. A. Moser and W. Scott have demonstrated,[1] there is no doubt of their tendency to concentrate in London, which is almost unique in this respect.[2] Indeed the evidence is that whilst commercial employment in London is expanding, commercial employment in the major provincial cities is failing to keep pace,[3] although it may be that the provincial cities will have a similar development boom to London at a later date.

The evidence of the London Traffic Survey[4] on internal journeys by land use and sources of attraction indicates that, whilst only 23 per cent of all journeys to all attractions within the survey area were to the central area, 62 per cent of total journeys to offices were to offices within the central area. This tendency towards centralisation of offices seems to arise from the high labour content of their output and the need for close personal contact. This pull forces

[1] *British Towns*, Oliver and Boyd, 1961.

[2] In 1962 central London had about 115 million sq.ft. of floor space, as compared with only 7 million sq.ft. in Manchester and Birmingham and 6 million sq.ft. in Liverpool.

[3] E. L. P. Hammond, 'The Main Provincial Towns as Commercial Centres', *Urban Studies*, November 1964.

[4] Freeman Fox and Partners *et al*, *London Traffic Survey*, Vol. 1, London County Council, 1964, especially Tables 6—26.

them towards the centre as the most accessible single point for personal travel for the whole city. For example, if a firm's employees are evenly spread over a circular area of radius r, mean journey distance (straight line) to the centre will be 0.67 r. To a point on the circumference, however, mean journey distance (straight line) will rise to 1.13 r. In the centre, offices can operate more successfully and profitably than most other forms of economic activity and land use. They thus tend to displace them. For not only are the costs of high office blocks[1] (compared with low) more favourable than for high blocks of flats (compared with houses), but high blocks do not have the inconvenience for office use that they have, say, for living. In fact they may gain from height, in daylight, reduction of street noise, privacy and prestige, and possibly in converting long horizontal journeys on foot to shorter vertical journeys on foot or by lift.

The advantages of high central blocks for offices is illustrated by the fact that, although maximum plot ratios (the ratio between permitted floor space and site area[2]) in London are 5.5,[3] much higher office blocks have been constructed in recent years, and it is unlikely that they have been built solely to gain external space at ground level.

The problem of decentralising office employment is almost unique to London, and, in view of the large expansion in office space in the centre, there is little doubt that planning controls have been ineffective in regulating the expansion of office employment—at least compared to the industrial development certificate. The Office Development Permit, introduced by the Control of Office and Industrial Development Act as from November 1964, may perhaps be more successful.

How far this failure has been due to weaknesses in the Town and Country Planning Acts and the burdens of compensation it is not as yet possible to say. One can only hope that these deficiencies have

---

[1] W. G. Holford, 'The Changing Face of London' in London: Aspects of Change, McGibbon and Kee, 1964.

[2] Although since this term expresses the (varying) ratio of floor space to the area of a given site, the term development ratio (or the earlier term floor space index) would be a more accurate description.

[3] J. B. Cullingworth, Town and Country Planning in England and Wales, Allen and Unwin, 1964.

been since rectified by the 1963 Act and the Control of Office and Industrial Development Act. Again of course planning controls cannot be used against existing office premises and employment without heavy burdens of compensation.

Since the controls to prevent development in congested central locations may be weaker, and are in any event virtually impossible to apply to existing premises, it is necessary to turn to the advantages and disadvantages of decentralisation as a possible influence in office dispersal. Here the advantages of concentration and centralisation become the disadvantages of dispersal. The strongest deterrent to even short-distance dispersal (within 100 miles of London) is fear of loss of contact with other firms, organisations and customers;[1] in general the advantages of dispersal in lower rents, better conditions for staff, and so on seem insufficient to compensate for this disadvantage. Also, as shown above, dispersal to a perimeter, with employees retaining their existing houses, is quite likely to lead to a net increase in personal mileage to be travelled so that the apparent net benefits to employees may be illusory; and there are substantial reasons for employees to retain their existing houses after a short-distance dispersal. It is true that many organisations have departments and routine operations which do not require external contacts, such as accounting, but separation of departments may nevertheless involve problems of communication and inconvenience within the firm. But these routine operations tend to be those which could be most easily mechanised, so that they may not in future account for a substantial proportion of the labour force.

In view of the advantages of centralisation and the disadvantages of dispersal of offices it is not surprising that experience so far, even on short distance dispersal of offices, has been somewhat disappointing, though recent results have been less so. The Economist[2] reported that many new office blocks remain unlet in suburban locations, with the exception of Croydon where good communications and the provision of a wide range of facilities have attracted some 6 million sq.ft. of office space, comparable in magnitude to the volume in Birmingham or Manchester.

At present, in spite of the temporary ban on office building within

[1] Location of Offices Bureau, *Annual Report 1963-4*, 1964.
[2] 4 April, 1964.

40 miles of London imposed in November 1964, it is possible that the centralisation of offices in London will continue to increase, for the LCC estimated that in 1963 planning permissions granted represented a commitment to an additional 25 million sq.ft., an eventual increase of about 22 per cent in central London office floor space.[1] This expansion was expected to result in 170,000 additional jobs in the next 5—10 years, but according to the Location of Offices Bureau[2] only about 40 per cent of this additional floor space was certain to materialise. It is doubtful whether office space and employment in the rest of Britain will increase as rapidly, in spite of control and the efforts of the Location of Offices Bureau, which it was hoped would eventually off-set the net inflow of new jobs by mainly short-distance dispersal.

Whatever the prospects for checking net expansion in office employment in London and in other cities, the prospects for dispersing the present concentrations, particularly in central London, are fairly remote.

Therefore, whilst it may be possible to disperse future *growth* in economic activity away from the main existing centres so that the latter will gradually reduce their share of total employment, it will be very difficult to disperse the existing centres without more substantial incentives and deterrents such as road pricing. There is a reasonable prospect that as existing manufacturing industry expands or renews premises, it will choose to disperse semi-voluntarily over a long period. For office employment, however, heavily concentrated in London, there seems to be no corresponding prospect of voluntary dispersal; the most it is possible to hope for is short-distance dispersal to cancel out future central growth.

Passing from private industry and normal economic activities to government, there remains the possibility of dispersing (with some degree of persuasion) about 100,000 civil servants in head-quarters staffs in London.[3] Some further dispersal is probably possible and is being pursued by government, but the linkages between departments of central government must be so close that

[1] Ministry of Housing and Local Government, *The South-East Study 1961–1981*, HMSO, 1964.

[2] *Op. cit.*

[3] Ministry of Housing and Local Government, *London; Employment, Housing, Land*, HMSO, 1963.

large-scale dispersal would probably demand the adoption or establishment of a new capital on the lines suggested by *The Economist* and other opinion-forming media. Although the suggestion may appear extreme it must be remembered that several nations—USA, West Germany, Canada, Australia, and many states in the USA—have capitals outside their major cities. Such are the pressures on London that this proposal demands serious consideration in spite of the obstacles.

SHOPPING TRENDS

An especially important service industry and one that can be expected to be more likely to decentralise than others is distribution. This fact arises primarily because it is an activity which is dependent on the distribution of the population. Being tied to the population no substantial or long-distance dispersal can of course be expected to take place but the scope for short-distance dispersal from existing town and city centres to suburbs and out-of-town shopping centres may be substantial and valuable to the solution of urban traffic and planning problems. In 1962 distributive trades accounted for 12.8 per cent of the insured population of Britain, almost 25 per cent of employment in the service industries, and it has also been one of the most expansionary activities, employment in distribution having increased by 34 per cent between 1952 and 1962.[1] It is therefore quantitatively important.

Unfortunately, although data on retail distribution from the censuses taken since 1950 is adequate, there is no information available on the geographical distribution of shopping floor space or other indicators. Trends between central and suburban shopping must therefore be inferred indirectly, and rather unsatisfactorily, from the performance of the kinds of shop which are located in central or non-central areas.

Censuses of Distribution suggest that current trends favour the larger shop which is normally located in town or city centres.[2] Thus among food shops the multiples (organisations with 10 or more shops) increased their share of turnover from 20.4

[1] M. F. W. Hemming, 'The Regional Problem', NIESR *Economic Review*, August 1963.
[2] Margaret Hall, 'Developments in British Retailing since 1957', *London—Cambridge Economic Bulletin: Times Review of Industry*, December 1963.

to 25.1 per cent between 1957 and 1961, whereas among non-food shops the multiples increased their share of turnover from 20.8 to 23.8 per cent. These multiples were the shops in which productivity per worker and innovation were proceeding most rapidly. However the evidence for increasing concentration in town centres is not entirely decisive, for in food shops the share of co-operatives declined (from 19.7 to 17.7 per cent) between 1957 and 1961, and among non-food shops the percentage share of department stores remained constant between the two dates.

Further factors tending to favour the larger shop and thus centralisation are the trends towards increasing expenditure on consumer durables with increasing income and the decline in resale price maintenance, which has been accelerated by the Resale Prices Act of 1964. Hitherto the smaller local shop has been protected from price competition from the generally more efficient larger shop; this process can be expected to continue over those areas of retail sales originally subject to resale price maintenance.

Finally, a trend favouring centralisation is the decline in the number of small shops in their traditional trades, e.g. grocery and food, which has been compensated by the growth of small specialist shops of a luxury character, pet shops, florists, photographic specialists, and so on. Since these are specialist shops catering for the infrequent demand of a large population, they tend to be located in town centres, whereas the traditional small shops were more localised.

While it must be accepted that recent trends have been towards shopping in town centres, this evidence is not decisive for the future because of opposing trends (e.g. mail order) and because hitherto public transport has been dominant in our cities, at least those with a population larger than about 100,000. But as car ownership spreads a change towards centralisation of shopping can be expected, if development controls allow.

The trends in towns of different sizes are likely to be somewhat complicated. The trend towards centralisation seems to arise from the large efficient unit like the supermarket, and, since they are only competitive when large populations are served, they must be sited in the centre of the smaller towns if they are to exist at all. Thus the trend in the smaller towns seems to be towards centralisation, retarded perhaps by congestion and lack of parking space.

In the larger towns and cities of over 100,000, suburban population and groupings around centres of good communication networks are likely to be large enough to sustain larger shops like supermarkets. Supermarkets, cars and refrigerators are natural allies in a trend towards once-a-week shopping with bulky loads, requiring the private car and plentiful and accessible parking space. This trend would be strengthened by urban road pricing and perhaps by growing congestion or traffic restrictions in city centres as the transfer from public to private personal transport continues.

Although centralisation of shopping is likely to continue in the smaller towns provided that road and parking facilities allow, there will nonetheless be a more even balance between centralising and decentralising forces in the larger towns and cities. Possibly decentralising forces may be more powerful, particularly if substantial local growths in population take place, giving opportunities for new shopping centres to be established with minimum risk.

TRANSPORT TRENDS

Transport is not an independent service but subordinate to other activities such as the location of economic activity, the desired densities of housing and the resultant distribution of the population. So even when a particular transport development favours decentralisation, the final outcome may be centralisation, decentralisation, or possibly no effect.

Concerning transport *per se*, however, there is no doubt that the dominant influences on dispersal or concentration are the economies and diseconomies of scale and the optimum size of unit. Where the optimum size is large as with the rail track, train or bus, the effect of a transfer to that type of transport will usually be centralising. On the other hand where it is comparatively small (e,g. the private car) a transfer to it will usually be decentralising. It is possible to analyse probable developments in terms of the well-known dichotomies between road and rail transport and public and private transport, but the effects must be analysed in terms of other classifications as well. We must for instance consider goods transport and personal transport with further sub-divisions for urban and rural (or interurban) trends; finally changes in modes of transport and the size of unit can be discussed.

Goods transport

The major change in goods transportation in recent years has been the change from rail to road: between 1954 and 1964 rail carryings fell from 22.1 to 16.0 thousand million ton-miles while carryings by road increased from 21.1 thousand million ton-miles to 38.5 thousand million ton-miles.[1] The forecasts of the Hall Committee[2] show that at the most optimistic estimate for the railways (4 per cent annual rate of increase in gross domestic product, equal shares with road in growth in carryings of general merchandise) rail carryings would only increase by 36 per cent over the 1961 level by 1980, whilst on the same assumptions ton-mileage by road was expected to increase by 130 per cent. In relative but not in absolute terms a further shift towards road transport is therefore likely.

To translate this general shift into an urban/rural division and into centralisation/decentralisation pressures requires some care. There is no doubt that the majority of goods ton-mileage is rural and inter-urban in character, but the growth of road transport is likely to have considerable urban effects, for while road goods transport almost always takes the form of a direct transfer from door to door, rail transport requires an urban railhead generally located near town centres. To avoid road congestion and make more profitable use of central sites, there is some pressure to decentralise urban rail goods facilities. It is evident then that the relatively higher rate of growth of goods transport, and the railways' response to it means that transport trends will probably continue to promote further decentralisation of urban industry. Like the transfer to road transport the process is already well advanced and may perhaps have little further to go.

Road pricing and goods transport

If urban road pricing were introduced the forces towards dispersal would be substantially strengthened. There is no reason to exclude goods vehicles from road pricing (see pp. 31 to 41 above), but difficulties would arise because of the lack of space-saving substitutes for urban road goods transport. Thus a pricing system would bear heavily on all industry in congested locations and on road goods

---

[1] Ministry of Transport, *Roads in England and Wales*, 1965.

[2] R. Hall et al., *The Transport Needs of Great Britain in the next 20 years*, HMSO, 1963.

transport in particular (at least during congested working hours). Industry could not be expected to undertake a large-scale re-location at all rapidly, or to endure hardship until it did so, so that a pricing system should be introduced only gradually for road goods transport, so that it had a small initial impact and yet progressively decentralising effects on all urban industry.

Personal transport

The most important sector for centralisation/decentralisation trends in personal transport is probably the urban, although rural trends will also be of some relevance. Rail travel, represented by passenger mileage on British Railways and on London Transport railways, has slightly declined from 24 thousand million passenger miles in 1954 to 23 thousand million passenger miles in 1964. During the same period passenger mileage by buses declined from 50 to 40 thousand million passenger miles. On the other hand the evidence is that private car traffic is increasing rapidly, from 47 to 126 thousand million miles from 1954 to 1964, an annual rate of increase of 11 per cent.[1] In very congested areas the increase in car traffic has probably been less than the national average; in central London for instance the annual rate of increase in car traffic was only about 4 per cent from 1952 to 1962.[2] These trends can be expected to continue if the capacity of road systems allows, and since capacity will normally be most adequate in rural areas, smaller towns and on the outskirts of congested areas, the trend towards the use of the private car will be decentralising *per se*.

The conclusion then is that both goods and personal transport trends are favourable towards dispersal, both of origins and destinations. The pattern of rail concentration and closures of lightly trafficked and duplicate lines will to some extent offset this development, and slightly increase the relative advantages of larger over smaller cities and conurbations.

THE PROSPECTS FOR DISPERSAL AND DECENTRALISATION

The above analysis of forces favouring concentration or dispersal of population and economic activity from our major cities, whose planning and traffic problems are most acute and intractable, can

[1] Ministry of Transport, *op. cit.*
[2] *Road Research 1963*, HMSO, 1964.

now be summarised. Housing preferences and costs favour dispersal at lower densities, and future trends in transport and shopping (with some reservations) likewise. Economic activity and sources of employment effects are different and more complex. The continuing decline in employment in agriculture and semi-rural industries such as mining and quarrying indicates some net transfer to urban employment; but its effect will probably be small in relation to existing levels of urban employment. More important are the trends in manufacturing and service industries. Employment in manufacturing industry is increasing least but is easier to disperse and more responsive to control; employment in services is rising faster but tending to concentrate, particularly on London. Moreover it has proved more difficult to control. Control or guidance can therefore do little to disperse existing concentrations of employment, although in the long run there is some prospect that manufacturing industry, aided perhaps by urban road pricing, will disperse semi-voluntarily when opportunities for doing so arise (e.g. renewal or expansion of building).

In urban areas we face continuing growth, pressure for dispersal of housing at lower densities and a tendency to attract service industries which usually concentrate in city centres and especially in London. The increasing separation between home and work-place, and the resulting urban and suburban spread, has become a common feature in recent years.

Since controls on industry, office employment and housing cannot disperse the existing concentrations of employment and economic activity, apart from the effects of road pricing, the most that can be hoped for is that future growth in population and employment will be dispersed by distributing population growth in the optimum manner, having regard to all the factors involved (e.g. people's preferences for housing, the difficulties in solving the traffic and planning problems of the larger towns and cities satisfactorily).

The distribution of the rising population
The problems of accommodating future urban population growth may be assessed as follows using the population distribution of England and Wales as an *example*. The population of England and Wales was expected by the office of the Registrar-General to grow

from the 46.1 million recorded in the 1961 census to about 65 million by the year 2000, a rate of increase slightly less than 1 per cent per annum. Even if the urban proportion does no more than remain constant, the numbers recorded as resident in urban areas can be expected to rise, from 36.8 million[1] to 51.8 million, an increase of 15 million in 40 years.

Normally accommodation of such an increase is approached by means of ad hoc proposals and expansions such as the South-East Study. But instead we shall examine the question more widely and systematically in terms of three main influences. These are (i) the distribution of the present urban population and the expansions required to accommodate an additional 15 million in urban population, (ii) the geographical distribution of the proposed expansions, and (iii) the political and institutional obstacles to expansion. The term expansion, of course, includes the establishment of new towns.

The distribution in 1961 of the urban population as officially defined is given in Table XI, all conurbations being grouped and regarded as single units.

It is evident from Table XI that the number of areas in which traffic and planning problems are likely to be very difficult is comparatively small. Thus there are only 40 separate areas with populations over 100,000 and only about 100 with populations of over 50,000, although these areas account for between 63 and 75 per cent of the total urban population. Correspondingly there are some 670 urban areas with populations less than 50,000 with easier traffic and planning problems, so that, for example, an expansion of 15 million in urban population could be achieved by expanding 300 of these towns by 50,000 or by expanding 600 of them by 25,000. Some part of these expansions would of course take place normally by natural increase.[2]

---

[1] This figure under-estimates the proportion living under urban conditions because quite large urban settlements are still regarded as rural districts, and the outskirts of many urban areas lie within rural districts.

[2] It should be noted that the conventional distinction between natural increase of the resident population in a given area and immigration cannot be made over a long period, because the immigrant population, tending to be young, will themselves contribute substantially to natural increase over a long period.

TABLE XI
Distribution of the Urban Population in England and Wales,
1961

Population 000's	No. of Areas	Cumulative Total	Aggregate Population 000's	% of total Population	Cumulative Percentage
Over 5,000	1*	1	8,172	22·2	22·2
4,000–5,000	0	1	0	0	22·2
3,000–4,000	0	1	0	0	22·2
2,000–3,000	2*	3	4,771	12·9	35·1
1,000–2,000	2*	5	3,089	8·5	43·6
500–1,000	1*	6	852	2·3	45·9
250–500	8	14	2,627	7·1	53·0
150–250	10	24	1,760	4·8	57·8
100–150	16	40	1,818	4·9	62·7
75–100	21	61	1,742	4·7	67·4
50–75	43	104	2,642	7·2	74·6
40–50	29	133	1,272	3·5	78·1
30–40	50	183	1,717	4·6	82·7
20–30	81	264	1,977	5·3	88·0
10–20	190	454	2,774	7·6	95·6
Less than 10	317	771	1,625	4·4	100·0
	771		36,838	100·0	

* Conurbations.

Source: Registrar-General, *1961 Census: Preliminary Report,* HMSO, 1963.

The optimum distribution of expansion

Against the background of Table XI and the need to accommodate a population increase of about 15 million, two main questions need to be answered. First, what is the best size of town to choose as a basis for expansion in physical and economic terms in the light of our objective of achieving a satisfactory and efficient final lay-out? Secondly, what is the best size of town from the viewpoint of attracting the 'requisite' volume of industry and other sources of employment?

On the first question it seems that, unless the larger towns or cities have some excess capacity in their basic installations (roads, water, drainage) taken as a whole (e.g. incremental cost of accommodating extra population falling appreciably), which is unlikely in view of their traffic and planning problems, the difficulties of expanding a town of substantial size efficiently and economically will be so great that the advantage must normally lie with expansions from a small base. In other words the new town, expanding from a small (or zero) population base, is so much easier to expand, construct and organise that unless larger towns offer genuine economies,[1] new towns must in general have the advantage.

As against this however seems to be the fact that industry and other sources of employment are in general reluctant to disperse to small towns with a narrow range of facilities, particularly the expanding service industries and offices on which the prospects for dispersal depend quite heavily. To quote the South-East Study[2] with its emphasis on decentralising office employment from London:

> 'The bigger the town the more chance there is of finding local industrial firms that could grow, given the necessary freedom and the stimulus of an expansion scheme.'
> 'There are other advantages. Generally speaking, the cost per head of providing basic services should fall with increasing size. And only the bigger towns—say 100,000 plus—can support a first-class shopping centre, a full range of urban services, a complete educational system and a variety of entertainments; these things are necessary not only in their own right, but also because they influence the decisions of employers.'

The South-East Study concluded with proposals for expansion:[3] three new cities one of which was to expand from 750,000 to 1,150,000 and two to expand from about 20,000 to about 170,000, five big expansions of 50,000 to 100,000 on bases ranging from 28,000 to 120,000, 12 expansions of at least 30,000 on bases ranging from 21,000 to 165,000, and one new town with various new town expansions.

Without fully accepting the conclusions of the study on the economics of expanding the larger towns, which already have substantial traffic and planning problems, and its views on new towns, weight must be given to the experience of the ministries

[1] The word 'genuine' is used as a warning that cost comparisons between new and expanded towns will be complex, e.g. they need to be at common and relevant price levels, and land values must be treated with care. Straight comparisons of expenditure on the two kinds of expansion are likely to be misleading therefore. The difficulties of expanding existing towns will be eased by broadly linear expansions on new sub-centres, rather than concentric expansion.

[2] *Op. cit.*, paras. 8 and 9.

[3] *Ibid.*, Table IV, p. 73.

concerned, and one must accept despite some reservations that the larger towns and cities will be the most attractive to industry and office employment.

Thus whilst the optimum size of base from which to expand in physical and economic terms is low, particularly for new towns, the optimum base from the viewpoint of attracting sources of employment is higher. There is a conflict of objectives. Reconciling this conflict suggests small or medium expansions on medium bases to a size which is not incompatible with the solution to traffic problems. But even when the problem is stated in these terms many alternative solutions are possible. For example, using the data in Table XI, and choosing a final population of 100,000 as the ceiling, some 250 towns, with present populations between 20,000 and 100,000, would need to be expanded by an average of 60,000 if a total increase of 15 million were to be accommodated. Alternatively, if a final population ceiling of 150,000 were chosen, some 160 towns with present populations between 30,000 and 150,000 would need to be expanded by an average of about 92,000.

Even before the geographical distribution of population expansion is considered and the political and institutional questions assessed, there is evidently a very wide range of issues to be settled and alternatives to be eliminated. More research, analysis and knowledge are required: some is supplied below.

Geographical distribution
Concerning the geographical distribution of population increase it is clear that the major pressures for dispersal will arise, indeed have arisen, in the conurbations, particularly in London and the South-East, where on recent trends the minimum population increase expected was at least $3\frac{1}{2}$ million (20 per cent) between 1961 and 1981.[1] Outside the London conurbation it is expected to double by the year 2000.

Although it is generally desirable for the solution of traffic problems and to ensure reasonable access to the countryside to disperse the population growth of the conurbations as far as possible, the fact must be faced that sources of employment will be reluctant to disperse to areas far from the major conurbations (e.g. beyond daily travelling distance). Much the same conflict between

[1] *The South-East Study, 1961—1981, op. cit.*

'normative' factors (i.e. what we ought to try to do) and the physical constraints upon them (what is likely to be possible) arises over distance as arose over population.

With the added constraint of distance from the conurbations, it is obvious that the suggestions made for dispersal above cannot be fulfilled, simply because many of the towns thought suitable for expansion will be too far from the large cities to attract industry and commerce. Also, with a combination of population and distance factors in dispersal, the range of alternatives becomes so wide that it seems one must perforce fall back on an *ad hoc* approach to dispersal. But it is possible to identify the areas of population pressure in England and thus, by exclusion, to indicate the areas apparently suitable for the reception of dispersed population.[1] An immediate problem is the choice of area; small areas are likely to be misleading because they may ignore spacious reception areas nearby, whilst a large area will conceal substantial internal variation. The region, broken down into counties where relevant, is chosen for the purpose of showing pressure areas as in Tables XII and XIII.

The four pressure areas with population densities above the national average may be grouped with possible reception areas as shown in Table XIII.

From these Tables the broad pattern of population pressure is that of a ridge running from London to the North-West and Yorkshire (with some significant gaps such as Oxfordshire) with natural reception areas to the east and west of this ridge.

Institutional problems

The political and institutional questions in dispersal arise because it seems essential that the strength of forces favouring local growth in population should outweigh opposition (except perhaps for new towns). But the interests of the individuals in the receiving area as variously interpreted by the local authority, public opinion and pressure groups, may be opposed to expansion and universal consent to public or private development may be impossible. Thus some interests may wish to preserve the character of an area which could be radically altered by expansion, particularly if they are retired people or have moved to a small town to avoid city

[1] For Scotland the pattern is simple: pressure in central Scotland, reception areas to north and south of centre.

TABLE XII

Population Pressures in England and Wales, 1961

Region	Population 000's	Density Persons/Acre	Annual Rate of Increase 1951–1961 %
London and S.E.	11,104	4·1	0·18
North-Western	6,567	3·0	0·18
East and West Riding	4,172	1·6	0·18
Midland	4,757	1·5	0·73
England and Wales	46,105	1·27	0·52
Southern	2,826	1·1	1·47
North Midland	3,634	0·9	0·73
Eastern	3,736	0·8	1·88
Northern	3,252	0·7	0·35
South-Western	3,411	0·6	0·55
Wales	2,644	0·5	0·17

Source: Registrar-General, 1961 Census: Preliminary Report, HMSO, 1963.

TABLE XIII

Groupings of Pressure and Reception Regions

Pressure Region	Reception Region	Remarks
London and South-Eastern	South-West (Wilts and Gloucs) Eastern (all counties except N. Herts and Essex) Southern (Hants and Oxon, western and northern fringes of Berks and Bucks)	Plus general dispersal over rest of Britain
North Western	N. Wales (Caerns. and Denbigh) East and West Riding* (West Riding terrain permitting) N. Midland (Derbys.)	Plus internal redistribution to Cheshire
*East and West Ridings	N. Midlands (Lincs.) Northern (North Riding)	Plus internal redistribution towards E. Riding
Midland	Mid-Wales	Plus internal redistribution to Shropshire and Herefordshire

* This region operates both as a pressure and a reception region, receiving from North-Western Region but dispersing to other regions.

life; others may object to an influx of outsiders of lower income or social status than themselves.[1] At the same time, shopping and other commercial interests may welcome an increase in population or the local authority may perhaps calculate that the gain to rate revenue will outweigh their additional costs, or genuine economies of scale may arise from a larger population if the existing population benefits from the larger range of services available in a larger town.

Some towns may face serious decline. Here the views of Dr G. P. Wibberley[2] on the economic and social role of the country town are relevant. After explaining how increased mobility and travel distances were tending to eclipse the traditional role of some country towns as marketing and distribution centres over a rough radius of 10 to 12 miles, he added:

> 'It is obvious therefore that many country towns have lost or are losing their original function. They will stagnate or decline unless some new function is found for them . . . Again many of the seemingly redundant country towns lie in locations suitable for the planned or unplanned dispersal of people from the large cities and conurbations'.

With external assistance and guidance, therefore, the political and institutional problems of dispersal may be minimised. As the successes of Croydon and Swindon have shown, direction and drive are very important to dispersal at the local authority level. Such a plan for national dispersal of industry would not necessarily conflict with priority for the less prosperous regions in location of industry, since this priority could be continued. But the existence of favoured alternatives to development districts might weaken their prospects of getting new industry, probably justifiably, for the policy of 'no expansion outside development districts' seems unduly rigid (see Chapter 2).

Dispersal by taxation
Various proposals for encouraging dispersal specifically by means of taxation rather than by planning and administrative action have been made, the most common being the pay-roll tax to be imposed

[1] Although insofar as the industrial growth to be dispersed is offices with employees of relatively high income and social status, opposition may be weak.

[2] 'The Economic and Social Role of the Small Country Town,' *Town and Country Planning*, October 1964.

on employers in congested areas as a tax per employee. A sophisticated system of pay-roll taxes and rebates has been proposed by
Messrs. Colin Clark and G. H. Peters.[1] The percentage rate of tax
would vary *directly* with the average population density within a
10-mile radius, with the total population within a 75-mile radius,
and *inversely* with the local unemployment percentage. If any of
these variables fell or rose above certain levels, the tax would be
transformed into a rebate.

Such taxes have the advantages of encouraging *all* existing
industry and commerce to disperse without burdens of compensation, but without detailed justification they will appear arbitrary
and unfair to the employer and employee, and it will be difficult
to gain their acceptance. Although road pricing was originally
proposed to reduce congestion, it will have similar advantages to
pay-roll taxes in encouraging dispersal of sources of employment.
But just because it is a 'tax on congestion' it will appear more
specific, less arbitrary, and be more acceptable than pay-roll taxes.
Therefore, although road pricing is not yet generally accepted and
is perhaps more difficult to impose and administer, on balance it
seems a preferable alternative to pay-roll taxes.

[1] 'Steering Employment by Taxes and Rebates', *Ekistics*, September 1964.
This is not of course to be confused with the Selective Employment Tax,
now under discussion.

CHAPTER 8

THE PLANNING PROCESS

PARTLY TO summarise the foregoing discussion and partly to clarify the process of planning which is at present evolving, it is useful to place the planning process in perspective. Initially however it is necessary to consider a common view and attitude to long-term urban planning, *that it necessarily aims to impose a grand design in some detail on an existing town or city. This attitude may be useful to inspire the planner and to sell his ideas to the public, but in most cases it must prove unrealistic. We only have the resources to transform our towns and cities substantially over a long period and cannot foresee the future accurately. Therefore the function of comprehensive planning must inevitably be more modest.* It is probably more realistic to regard it as the process of trying to foresee the lines along which future changes and investments could best be made, the process of physical change being so slow that circumstances and knowledge will almost certainly change and require a new plan long before the original plan can be carried out. Thus, in a real and somewhat frustrating sense long-term comprehensive plans can be little more than a guide, an attempt to identify a shifting target: they cannot and *should not* be fully implemented. The need for flexibility and change in plans and in their execution is obvious and, if manageable, a matrix of alternative assumptions and solutions should perhaps be presented on lines being evolved by Dr P. A. Stone at the National Institute of Economic and Social Research.

A MODEL OF CURRENT TRENDS IN A 'TYPICAL' CITY

To analyse planning more closely, let us consider a typical town or city. In a literal sense of course there is no such thing as a typical town or city, but there are sufficient common features to make the idea of a typical town or city comprehensible. In this typical town or city, say of 100,000 population, we have the centre, the most attractive and accessible single point to the whole population where land values and densities are high and from which intensive users of *ground* space, offices, certain shops, tend to displace the less intensive users such as industry and housing, although some higher density housing on the less accessible floors is competitive. Although buildings are often old in the centre of towns there is considerable commercial incentive to improve, adapt, or to renew them *individually* (more recently on a more comprehensive scale) and the main deficiencies lie within the public sector—roads, lay-out, parking and environment. It is also in the centre that most of the historic buildings or buildings of architectural interest are normally found.

Around the centre lies an area of mixed development consisting of uses displaced from the centre (garages, industry, transport installations), but largely of pre-1921 twilight housing at high densities of 20 to 30 dwellings to the acre. Rateable values, incomes and car ownership are low in what might be termed this 'twilight ring'. Outside the twilight ring lies what might be termed the 'modern ring' where housing tends to be newer, residential densities progressively fall to an average of about five dwellings to the acre, and incomes, car ownership and rateable values are progressively higher.

In this typical city, what problems have arisen and what are the alternative solutions to these problems and the costs of each alternative? First of all, the city has grown since its centre was established and at the same time it has probably become more centre-oriented with increasing mobility in the sense that a larger proportion of journeys are to the centre. Secondly, means of transport have changed, and although the city has probably always been congested by slow-moving traffic and speeds may actually be rising, the disparity between the desired and actual speeds of vehicles has probably widened substantially. Thirdly, encouraged by growth in income per head, higher car ownership and increased mobility, families and housing are pressing to spread at lower densities, partly resisted by planning controls. Finally, for the reasons outlined above, there is a demand, behind which are commercial and political pressures, to renew and redesign town centres. There will also be a desire to renew the twilight ring, although because of the distortions and imperfections of the housing market outlined in Chapter 6, and the comparative poverty or contentment of home-owners or inhabitants, there will be little commercial or financial support for this objective, except perhaps at high densities (where permitted) or in more profitable uses than housing.

The main problems and opportunities then arise in the town centre and in the twilight ring; they demand some renewal and a new lay-out to achieve equilibrium between the conflicting objectives of lay-out, means of transport, traffic, together with segregation to avoid conflict and to protect the environment.

The achievement of equilibrium

Equilibrium may be achieved physically by expanding the road system to accommodate *all* traffic, or by dispersing and de-centralising the main central 'attractors', or by a combination of both means. To some extent the growth in car ownership and the general desire to live at low densities will encourage dispersal and de-centralisation but sources of employment will probably not show the same natural tendency to disperse, particularly the growth sector offices.

In the present state of knowledge, it is difficult to discern how this long-term equilibrium between traffic and people's other wants (e.g. for living space) on the one hand, and urban lay-out on the other, can be achieved, but it is nevertheless important to hazard the attempt. High car ownership at the levels suggested by Buchanan will only take place, on Beesley's and Kain's evidence,[1] at lower densities than are normal in British cities, for instance in those high density 'twilight' areas near the town centre: among the residents in these areas will be a large proportion of the forecast increase in car owners—if it is to come at all—simply because of their numbers and present distance from saturation level in car ownership.[2] Thus increased car ownership to the levels forecast by Buchanan and residential dispersal or de-centralisation at lower

---

[1] M. E. Beesley and J. F. Kain, 'Urban Form, Car Ownership and Public Policy: An Appraisal of Traffic in Towns', *Urban Studies*, November 1964.

[2] For example, in the London Traffic Survey (Table 5—16) some 1,700,000 households with present incomes below £1,500 per annum did not have cars in 1962: above a household income of £1,500 per annum, only about 145,000 households did not have cars.

densities will normally tend to occur together, and as a natural corollary, dispersal or de-centralisation of the central attractors by planning, pricing and by other methods will be necessary. Such a process will naturally achieve equilibrium; but at what level of car ownership and use, utilisation of public transport, restriction of traffic, it will or should occur is of course impossible to predict.

Equilibrium, whether achieved by market forces or planning, will have important implications. First, cities will tend to become less centre-oriented, thus making the accommodation of traffic more manageable. Secondly, existing cities will tend to spread at lower densities consequent on de-centralisation. Thirdly, a policy of dispersal of population to distant smaller towns from major cities and conurbations will be vital to secure an efficient distribution of the population.

LONG-TERM PLANNING IN DETAIL

The growth in motor traffic and plans, and adjustments to them, take many years so that prediction over a long period is necessary. But unforeseen changes within this period are inevitable and certain to be substantial; the probability of error is high. To make a realistic, detailed long-term plan is therefore impossible and any 40-year end-of-century plan cannot be more than tentative and general. Details should be filled in by shorter-term 5- or 10-year development plans and only on the latter should firm policy and detailed financial commitments be made along the lines indicated in Chapters 4 and 5;[1] investment constraints on both long- and short-term plans will of course be necessary for the sake of realism.

A broad long-term 40-year plan will be difficult to accommodate to current planning techniques, since the latter attempt a detailed, factual and scientific approach. Current procedure is roughly as follows. The firm starting point is a land use/transport survey whereby the urban survey area is as far as possible divided into homogeneous zones (in terms of land use and other relevant characteristics).[2] The existing volumes of traffic between zones can be established by home interviews on the journeys and on the economic and social status of households. These estimates are

[1] Short-term plans are not of course immune from error, but they reduce the possibilities of inaccurate prediction.

[2] These surveys are a very substantial and rapidly changing subject in their own right, the details of which can only be touched upon here.

checked and verified by assignments to the existing road system and by measurements of traffic flow.

Then we come to the problem of prediction for 40 years ahead. This forecast will consist of two elements: first, the growth of traffic arising from more car ownership and from other predicted changes in transport on the *existing pattern of land use*, and second, the expected *changes* in land use. Changes in car ownership in each zone may be predicted by deriving existing relationships between car ownership and other independent variables including income, social status and residential density. This relationship may be in the form of a multiple regression equation which attempts to express car ownership in terms of the most relevant (and most predictable) variables. Since many of the possible variables are closely correlated, this equation can assume many possible forms. Perhaps the most significant kind of relationship is suggested by the equation derived by Beesley and Kain from American data[1] and applied to car ownership in Leeds:

$$A = 148.75 - 0.0084\,D + 0.03455\,Y$$

where A = no. of cars per 1,000 population in 1961,

D = population per sq.mile of land in urban use for whole city,

Y = median family income in 1961 in dollars.

Predictions of car ownership from survey data will generally be lower than the Buchanan/Road Research Laboratory prediction of 0.4 cars per head by the year 2010, since the latter is a national prediction for urban and rural areas alike, tacitly assuming that residential and other densities would be no deterrent to increase in car ownership (see Chapter 5). For example, as compared with the Buchanan forecast of 0.4 cars per head for Leeds in 2010, using the above equation and assuming an exchange rate of $3.41 to the £ (giving parity in purchasing power) Beesley and Kain forecast an ultimate car ownership of only 0.258 per head at existing densities, slightly reduced to line up with Buchanan's assumptions.

Positive and normative stages in planning

Finally, future growth in car ownership and other changes in transport are translated into trips generated from each zone by deriving and applying regression equations from the survey itself,

[1] *Op. cit.*

and the trips allocated between zones by the various known methods to give the expected *future* pattern of traffic on the existing pattern of land use.

Future changes in land use are considered next, and here it must be emphasised that if planning and transport are to be in 'balance', it will generally be necessary to devote fully as much attention to changes in land use as to changes in transport, particularly the location of the central attractors which are critical to the plan and to the future working of the town; the use of home interview techniques has the possible effect of deflecting attention from the attractors. Changes in land use will consist partly of realistic elements (i.e. what is likely to happen), and partly of normative elements (i.e. what ought to happen in the interests of 'good planning' and efficient lay-out).

To cover the realistic elements, changes in population must be predicted together with the economic future of the city; here one is forced to rely upon the *National Plan* and other detailed growth models of the economy, translated down into regional and local terms. This procedure will involve considerable estimation and guesswork. Then the location (and density) of housing for population growth, residential renewal, and for any overspill population arising from renewal, must be provisionally decided, together with the locations of the various expected types of economic activity. Finally, the ultimate traffic flows between zones must be predicted, new forecasts of car ownership and trip generation being necessary for any changes in residential density consequent on renewal.

These predicted changes in land use, traffic and density must then be incorporated and translated into a provisional plan which is initially traffic-dominated in the sense that it will be mainly concerned with the broad design and costs of road networks to accommodate ultimate traffic volumes.

The normative aspect of planning must then take over. That is to say, the provisional long-term plan must be reviewed as a whole to decide whether it is the best possible plan for the city within all the relevant physical, economic and aesthetic constraints. The major questions that must be asked and answered at this stage are as follows. Is it possible to accommodate all the traffic that will arise in the centre and if not at what level and by what method (restraint, pricing or decentralisation) should equilibrium be achieved? Is each expected land use in its optimum location in relation to other considerations and land uses? In answering the latter question the main decisions to be taken relate to the central attractors and their location. Detailed knowledge of their space-utilisation characteristics (e.g. intensive or extensive user of *ground* space) and the pattern of transport attracted to them will be necessary in order to consider re-planning their location, together with information on the physical state of buildings and future trends in the relevant industry or activity. There is little doubt that many if not most of the central attractors will apparently be pulled towards the centre as the general point of minimum total transport costs for the whole urban population; this is after all the cause or effect (or both) of their central location. Those uses whose 'transport-pulls' towards the centre are effect rather than cause of their central location can be considered as candidates for relocation, and some uses may be survivals with a weak case for a central location. Also a central location with today's traffic conditions may by no means be appropriate at future levels of traffic. In effect each central attractor should be debited with the costs of congestion imposed on other users attributable to the traffic it attracts,[1] or in the long term the costs of accommodating the traffic it attracts. Its possible re-location should be planned accordingly, either directly or by encouraging development and competition from better-located substitutes.

By such means as these a final long-term plan incorporating decisions on lay-out, road network, environmental areas, etc. may be evolved, but as yet it is not possible to offer anything like complete general guidance. A formidable amount of work and research remains to be done before town planners can be reasonably sure that these techniques will be sufficient to guide us to the best long-term plan for any given town or city, and as far as possible planning should be a research exercise rather than the application of set techniques.

[1] These costs may be substantial, for from Chapter 2 it can be estimated that a single commuter by car travelling 10 miles a day in an urban area at an average speed of 15 m.p.h. may impose costs of £150 per annum on other road users. Similarly the costs of accommodating such a commuter satisfactorily in terms of extra road capacity may approximate to £1,000 in capital costs, plus a further capital cost of £1,000 for off-street parking.

In view of the complex sequence outlined above the suggested steps towards the evolution of a long-term plan are summarised as follows; the first of the short-term plans follows, and does not precede, the long-term plan:

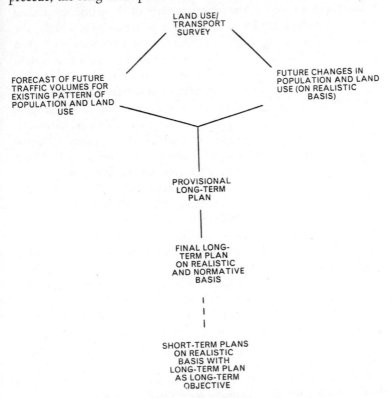

FIGURE 6 THE EVOLUTION OF A LONG-TERM PLAN

One fact which may be held to save this system of planning from impossible complexity is that some of the decisions to be made are not critical. Many alternative courses of action will have little effect on the final outcome and some errors can be rectified or compensated by subsequent changes in planning policy. It is therefore vital to identify both those decisions which are non-critical, for example peripheral questions, and those which are critical. Amongst the latter are all factors affecting the town centre, the capacity and design of the central road network, of which the frequency of intersections is the most critical.

The need for simplification

Although every step in the above outline of the planning process seems essential, justifiable and at any rate tentatively soluble, the total procedure is in reality so extensive and intricate that even with the aid of computers and other advanced techniques it is hard to see more than a few people being able to solve the problems in a reasonable time, and few more able to understand their solutions.

The tacit assumption of present planning trends is that if only enough facts are collected and analysed to establish relationships, they may then be summed or multiplied to predict human behaviour and choices and the appropriate long-term technical and economic responses. Yet, although any single step or series of steps may be valuable, there nonetheless comes a point when the final analysis becomes remote from reality, too large and too abstract to be trustworthy. What check have we *now* on the accuracy of long-term 40-year physical plans and predictions? Can the planning process really simulate the workings of the economic system, itself the result of many millions of largely subjective decisions which so far can only be given objective expression by a device such as the price mechanism?

Perhaps fortunately few minds can stay on such a level of abstraction for long and already a simpler solution to town planning and transport problems is emerging, although it would be hard to prove and justify it as yet.

Assuming a typical city (population more than, say, 100,000), the developing solution seems to have three elements:

(i) Assuming suburban trunk road or motor-way approaches to the city, a terminal ring around the city at a point where present mean traffic journey speeds fall below 15-20 m.p.h.[1] This road would act as a high speed distributor and a reasonably cheap and effective alternative, to minimise travel in the more congested area within the ring, on the lines put forward by Dr Smeed.[2]

---

[1] If the city is expected to grow substantially in population and size, this ring may need to be built further out.

[2] R. J. Smeed, 'The Traffic Problem in Towns,' *Manchester Statistical Society*, 8 February, 1961.

(ii)   Within the ring a sensitive system of direct road pricing by on-vehicle meters with charges varying with vehicle mileage, type of vehicle, and resultant degree of congestion.[1] Pricing in this way will give an incentive to use the ring route.

(iii)   At a later date, perhaps towards the end of the century, if traffic volumes, pricing revenues, road investment resources and development opportunities permit, construction of a rectangular grid system of primary motorways within the ring, demarcating a system of environmental areas.[2] Road pricing of course should be maintained, but adjusted to the new degree of congestion.

This programme would not only have substantial effects in both accommodating and restraining traffic. It would also have a dispersive effect on central land uses that attract large volumes of traffic, which would be encouraged to disperse to near the ring and beyond. In addition, although the problem of excessive city growth may not be solved, such a system, by rectifying the omission of market forces from current planning, may relieve much of the pressure on, and restrictive effects of, controls,[3] and allow planning to resume the moderately regulative and design functions which is what it can do most efficiently.

It may be objected to this solution that it depends critically upon road pricing, which may prove politically unacceptable. But the probable alternative is restraint by congestion which will certainly not prove popular! Road pricing is in any case economically superior, even though intolerable levels of congestion are unlikely. (See above, p. 68.)

SOME PITFALLS AND ERRORS

The problems raised by comprehensive and fundamental long-term planning are formidable and have not as yet been solved. As a supplementary aid it may therefore be valuable to emphasise the pitfalls and what should *not* be done.

In the first place, it is important to approach the long-term plan as far as possible without pre-conceived ideas on the details of design,

---

[1] *Road Pricing: The Economic and Technical Possibilities*, HMSO, 1964.

[2] *Piccadilly Circus: Report of the Working Party*, HMSO, 1965.

[3] D. J. Reynolds, 'Planning, Transport and Economic Forces,' *Journal of the Town Planning Institute*, November 1961.

architecture, the importance of the town centre and so on.[1] Otherwise it is likely that the plan will be arbitrarily fitted to these
preconceptions. Any plan of course is subject to genuine constraints
on the planner's freedom of action—some historic buildings must
be preserved, newer buildings may not be worth demolishing and
re-building, and geographical features also delimit the sphere of
decision-taking. It is the more important that artificial constraints
should not be built into plans and all relevant variables must be given
their due weight without bias.

In the second place, it is necessary to avoid false antitheses which
are common in planning and which create apparent but unreal
methodological conflicts. One such is that between what are termed
'human values' on the one hand and the more materialistic manifes-
tations of human behaviour such as the private car and the supermarket. Apart from the fact that the term 'human values' and its
variants are too vague and all-embracing to be meaningful, it must
be pointed out that almost all the physical factors in planning are
the result, directly or indirectly, of personal choices which,
however misguided they may be held to be, are still 'human'
and 'valuable'. Again, the antithesis between 'human' or aesthetic
values and 'financial gain' is at least partly false and irrelevant
because 'financial gain' is only possible if the profit-seeker himself
serves individual choices and preferences as registered in the demand
for his product. There is no obvious reason (given road pricing,

---

[1] In discussions on urban transport and planning it is common to emphasise
the difficulties of accommodating traffic in town centres, yet to insist that
traffic is vital to the 'prosperity' of the town centre, and that the town
centre must remain 'prosperous'. This inconsistency in attitude must be
resolved. There seems no fundamental reason why town centres should
remain 'prosperous'; after all, if town centres in their concentration and
lay-out are unsuitable to present and future demands or techniques,
decline and dispersal of town centres seems desirable. Past capital
invested in town centres does not determine their real *present* value, which
depends on their efficiency in meeting *future* demands. Nor should planning
controls be used to protect existing enterprises from competition, even
though some element of monopoly is inevitably imposed upon them by
such controls.

Another odd aim in planning is to avoid decline in rateable *values*,
particularly in town centres. This could of course be compensated by a
corresponding change in rate *poundages* without increasing the overall rate
burden. Electoral considerations presumably inhibit this.

etc. and with reasonable design control) why the motive power of 'financial gain' should produce socially undesirable results; every development must be judged on its merits and not assessed by the motives of its sponsors, which are largely irrelevant to physical planning.

A common and seriously misleading antithesis is that between 'human values' on the one hand and statistics or quantitative methods on the other. The idea is that statistics are inhuman—'We plan for people not statistics'. Statistics and quantitative methods can be over-done, but *in the absence of markets* they are often the only way to discover people's real wants and preferences in a complex situation (as shown by their behaviour and choice). Avoidance of statistics and quantitative methods in this situation therefore generally means the substitution of a subjective judgement of people's wants and preferences which may be seriously in error. Many aspects of planning cannot be quantified but this is no reason to reject those that can. On the other hand, as has been emphasised, where pricing is possible it is generally a more accurate and more efficient indicator of consumers' requirements than even the best statistical substitutes.

A more serious and genuine conflict may arise between aesthetic values and the requirements of efficient lay-out; the lay-out needed to accommodate traffic efficiently may overwhelm the pedestrian and be generally regarded as ugly or impersonal. This conflict can be partly resolved by conceding the case for the retention of, and proper setting for, buildings of architectural or historic interest. In long-term planning it may generally be done more easily because the larger the scale of redevelopment considered, the more freedom there is for decisions on the location and detailed design of individual buildings or roads. Each building therefore appears less of an obstacle to the success of the plan.[1] Partly too it might be met by giving pedestrian distances and delays due weight in road and planning policies.

However conflict between aesthetics and efficiency may not finally be eliminated by such concessions, and it may often be

---

[1] For example, assuming that all new developments are square in shape, an isolated building to be retained in the centre of a ¼-acre square plot will inhibit all developments over 1/16th acre in size, whereas in the centre of a 1-acre plot only developments over ¼-acre in size will be inhibited.

judged necessary to alter the most efficient lay-out for the sake of aesthetic appeal. But it remains important to work out the most efficient lay-out *initially* and then to make aesthetic concessions or additions; only in this way can the necessary decisions be made clear and the costs of the various alternatives be calculated.

A further pit-fall to be avoided if possible is the use of general standards, of (say) density or open space. Although these may be a useful general guide (never to be exactly applied in any given instance) in the absence of better information, the aim must always be to obtain the answer or result appropriate to the situation; general standards may be arbitrary or inappropriate.

A final example of what not to do in planning is the *deus ex machina* approach. That is to say, having been confronted almost inevitably with a difficult problem, the planner is tempted to seize upon a solution without adequate reasoning or full appraisal and criticism of the solution. Favourites for this kind of treatment are new means of public transport (the mono-rail, the helicopter or the hover-craft) and the linear city, although, perhaps significantly, few of these ideas have ever been tried out and adopted on any scale. This is not, of course, to decry the merits of new ideas, new means of transport or linear cities which may sometimes prove the right solution. It is a warning against the uncritical methods by which they have often been selected or proposed. The deficiencies of planning do not lie in a dearth of ideas, but in a lack of systematic method and discipline for their evaluation (see Chapter 9).

CONCLUSIONS:

POSSIBLE SOLUTIONS TO THE URBAN PLANNING PROBLEM

THIS WORK has examined four major town planning problems: the general planning problem (in which the questions of regional and urban/rural balance are dominant), the accommodation of traffic in towns, urban renewal, and the accommodation of a rising urban population.

Not surprisingly no simple answers or easy techniques have emerged; indeed part of the value of a wide survey and analysis is to show that the four problems are closely inter-related. In fact there is no question of solving the urban traffic problem or pressing on with urban renewal itself; all four sets of problems must be solved simultaneously and this makes the task of town planning peculiarly difficult, while at the same time opening up certain opportunities.

If there is any key to the solution of these problems it lies mainly in dispersal and decentralisation of economic activities (particularly those attracting large volumes of traffic). Dispersal and decentralisation will clearly encounter obstacles of their own however, and equilibrium must inevitably take place on many margins.

POLICIES FOR DECENTRALISATION

Decentralisation and dispersal may take several forms:

(1) *Expansion of town centres to accommodate the present uses or attractors at lower densities.* Even a modest expansion of town centres could have substantial effects on reducing congestion and making the accommodation of traffic easier. Such modest dispersals would have little adverse effect on activities which were strongly pulled

towards centres, and could often be undertaken by re-developing adjacent twilight areas. The net compensation payable for the acquisition of premises vacated on decentralisation might also be a manageable problem, because planning authorities could offer cheaply acquired but attractive sites in twilight areas in exchange for costlier central sites.

(2) *Decentralisation of central uses to the outskirts of towns.* This policy has obvious attractions for town planning and may be attractive to some uses, industry in particular. So many central uses are strongly pulled towards the centre, as the point of minimum total transport costs for the whole town, that the movement is likely to encounter resistance. Nevertheless road pricing, if it can be imposed, will aid decentralisation and will be amply supported by the growth in car ownership, congestion, decline in public transport and encouragement of dispersed competitors, e.g. out of town shopping centres.

(3) *Dispersal of existing population and economic activity from the larger cities and conurbations to smaller towns at some distance from them.* To a certain extent this population pattern is already appearing semi-voluntarily, but the dispersal of economic activity is retarded because manufacturing industry, being more mobile, is least likely to expand, whilst services and offices (particularly in London) are more expansionary and an important cause of centralisation.

(4) *Dispersal of population growth to new and expanded towns.* Broadly speaking the areas of high population pressure lie between London in the south-east and the Lancashire and Yorkshire conurbations in the north, with low pressure reception areas to the east and west of this ridge Although new towns have fundamental advantages for the reception of 'overspill' population, the scale of population growth is likely to require towns to expand on a substantial scale. Here broad linear expansions on new sub-centres to avoid further over-loading of town centres are indicated, at least for the larger expanded towns where traffic and planning problems will be most critical.

Research into dispersal and road pricing
A programme of research into the possibilities and policies for dispersal seems desirable, and in view of obstacles to dispersal it is

natural to look for general semi-automatic instruments such as taxes
or subsidies to encourage it. Although pay-roll taxes have much to
commend them, they appear more arbitrary than taxes specifically
expressing the costs of congestion such as road pricing. At least
therefore some simple initial experiments in road pricing should
be made.

Such a simple experiment could be as follows. A fairly isolated
town should be chosen (to avoid the complications and fears of
competition from nearby centres) with a good by-pass system
allowing through traffic to avoid charges without serious hardship.
Then within the town and the surrounding county(ies) the annual
car licence fee (£17 10s.) would be waived, and motorists charged
(say) 1s. per day, and an approximately proportional levy over a
year, to enter the town within the by-passed area. In this way few
people could argue that they were substantially worse off. The results
of the experiment would be valuable not only to the case for road
pricing but also in revealing what is at present unknown—the
importance attached by users to the car and the case for urban
road investment. Other more complex experiments could follow.

The key to the solution to the urban planning and traffic problems
then lies in gradual guided dispersal, aided by the semi-automatic
instrument of road pricing and by ring routes and such other
investments as appear to be justified by revenues from road pricing,
congestion and other relevant criteria. Though there are obstacles
to this solution, the problems of relying on 'planning' alone appear
much more formidable—no clear guide-lines or criteria, an
irreducible range of competing alternative solutions, the intransigent
problems of predicting the distant future, heavy costs of reconstruction and all the familiar consequences of trying to operate against
'market forces', the immediate demands of many people with
individual interests, pressures and problems which make it unlikely that they will ever give much direct weight to planning.

PROBLEMS IN PLANNING

The dominant theme in this analysis has been the difficulties and
limitations of planning. They have been emphasised not to induce
pessimism, but to clarify the problems and the conflicts and try to
remove them. The planning machine, although it may be admired
for its administrative framework, is, both in the quantity of per-

sonnel and the quality of its techniques, at present inadequate to deal with the problems facing us.

In part the present inadequacies of town planning arise from history and the varying pressures of planning problems. With a history of 60 or 70 years in Britain, planning only matured to something like our present system in 1947-8, and after a brief period of activity, it declined and was given little weight during the 1950s when the problems of traffic, population increase, regional imbalance and so on were building up, somewhat unexpectedly. Consequently it is hardly surprising that the machine is unequal to the load and that there is a shortage of planners (which could be met, be it noted, partly by simplifying and clarifying the subject).

This shortage has meant that staff has been largely engaged on development control and other pressing *ad hoc* problems rather than on planning as such. This has not only weakened planning but must have been wasteful in that many related and over-lapping developments were separately investigated, whereas more fundamental planning would have enabled sounder decisions to have been made at less cost.[1]

Many planning authorities have staffs so small that they cannot specialise and it is extraordinary that some central body to advise local authorities and conduct research has not been set up. The Republic of Ireland with a population of only 2.8 million and with relatively modest planning problems compared with our own, has established a National Institute for Physical Planning and Research. And even our Road Research Laboratory, probably with smaller (though still difficult) problems[2] to tackle, had a staff of 500 and an annual budget of £1 million in 1964.

Thus town planning at the moment is often incapable of using the more quantitative techniques necessary to work closely with traffic engineers and economists.[3] Town planning techniques lag behind and seem incompatible with the methods used for the solution of traffic problems.

[1] D. L. Foley, *Controlling London's Growth*, University of California Press, 1963.
[2] The most difficult transport problem, urban traffic, is of course common to road research and planning.
[3] C. D. Foster, 'Economics, Town Planning and Politics', *Journal of the Institute of Transport*, January 1965.

This gap raises the formidable problems of how to train planners and what disciplines they should be taught. It is arguable whether there can be a distinct homogeneous profession such as planning, because the term at present covers a heterogeneous range of subjects—housing, location of industry and of economic activity, and transport, among others—and a broad range of basic disciplines such as architecture, engineering, surveying, geography, economics and sociology. Because of the impossibly wide range of knowledge *and* depth of understanding required of the planner, it is currently accepted by some that planning must be done by groups of specialists including architects, engineers and traffic engineers.[1] But this team approach is not entirely satisfactory because it demands too much from the team leader in reconciling different contributions; there are awkward 'language barriers' between the different specialisations, particularly between the visual, non-quantitative, intuitive approach and the quantitative and scientifically-based disciplines.

Remedies for these difficulties, which are inherent in planning, are not easy but the following are suggested. First, the profession seems to demand dominance of the pure planner with a training as such in the wide range of subjects and disciplines required. It is true that this training will involve a long course and demand a race of super-men if planning is not clarified and simplified, but it will help to ensure that planners owe loyalty in their outlooks and techniques to the requirements of town planning rather than to those derived from another profession. It should be noted that of the membership of the Town Planning Institute in 1959, 45 per cent also held membership in the parent profession of architecture, 21 per cent in engineering, 12 per cent in surveying and 2 per cent in landscape architecture. The representation of economics was and is negligible.

Under the dominance of the pure planner it is necessary of course to continue and refine the contribution of the specialist, but to differentiate planning clearly and so reflect the wide internal differences. Professions trained in the more subjective aspects of planning should concentrate on and strengthen them, leaving the objective, quantitative aspects to professions trained in handling

[1] A. Ling, 'Technical and Professional Problems of Redevelopment', *Journal of the Town Planning Institute*, July/August 1964.

them, and thus to strengthen *them*. A proposed differentiation is given in Table XIV, the economist incidentally playing something of a border-line rôle between the objective and subjective aspects.

TABLE XIV
Proposed Division of Planning

Planning Sector	Professions and Specialisations Required	Area of Planning to be Covered
Planning	Pure planner, geographer, traffic engineer, engineer, mathematician, operational research worker, statistician, economist, demographer.	Research; development of theory and techniques; drawing up of regional plans and town plans in broad quantitative terms, not in detail.
Architect/ Planning	Architect/planner, architect, landscape and townscape architect, traffic engineer, engineer, economist.	Detailed planning; design and lay-out of buildings, roads, etc. and their proper setting; the environment; aesthetic questions; research.
Social Planning	Sociologist, psychologist, architect, architect/planner.	Surveys to discover people's wants; design of lay-outs and buildings to enhance personal and social life.
Administration of Planning	Pure planner, architect/ planner, traffic engineer, engineer, administrator, economist, lawyer.	Development control; decision-making; practical applications; day-to-day work.

Whatever division is organised urban planning must be substantially altered if it is to cope with present problems adequately and systematically. In particular it must develop from a semi-quantitative, semi-artistic subject where conventions and fashions (based on little or no evidence or research) predominate, to a more quantitative, cost-orientated subject in which economic and scientific methods are dominant, leaving the more subjective aspects of planning to specialised sub-divisions. The unnecessary mixture of objective and subjective elements in planning seems likely to weaken the quality of both. It is doubtful whether planning, which is mainly an administrative, technical, economic and political process, can ever serve aesthetic ends effectively; architects and aesthetes can best do battle on their own ground.

This proposed revolution in outlook and methods is a sizeable task and not likely to be completed in a short time; no adequate body of theory, techniques or practice[1] has yet been evolved and the impulse must come first from fundamental research, related to the general problems and *not* just to particular schemes and *ad hoc* proposals. Such new techniques as are evolved must be taught and a new species of planner evolved. This process should be aided by the incursion of specialists from other related fields—transport, location of industry or geography—and from professions not normally associated with planning, such as economists or mathematicians, who are more accustomed to processing and interpreting data meaningfully and precisely. (Of the 100 or so references in this work, only 30 or so came from sources directly connected with town planning.) The potential contribution of related fields of study and action is probably considerable, particularly the processing of land use/transport surveys, and contributions from university departments, especially economists and geographers, who are currently expanding their interest in planning.

But the major problem in town planning remains that it has been, and is, trying to do too much; in practice it is trying to do the impossible, partly because it is called upon to rectify many of the distortions and omissions arising elsewhere. In the past town planners have worked largely through subjective judgement and hunch with little reference to prices, costs, wants or preferences, and have undertaken too little quantitative analysis and research. As it is at present evolving, town planning seems likely to become too complex for its problems to be soluble: the problems must therefore be simplified. Instead of trying to do things the vague or the hard

---

[1] The new town is a significant exception, in spite of controversy over detailed designs and lay-outs. There seems no reason why new towns, or villages, should not be privately as well as publicly developed, for the first new towns were private developments, and the 'new village' by Span Developments Ltd. at Hartley in Kent is of some interest. Private new towns or villages should be of value and interest as they should be able to devote more attention to the ultimate residents' wants, and appeal to a wider range of residents than publicly developed new towns, which almost inevitably select most residents from council housing lists.

way planning should be grouped, it is suggested, around the discipline of economics, which attempts to link the objective and subjective through the price mechanism. It could then be more systematically organised, less complex, and could concentrate on the regulative and design functions which are its strengths.

This proposal does not of course mean a dismantling of physical controls or a decline of planning activity. Central authorities must continue to provide a guiding function, a legal and institutional framework, and attempt to look into the future to anticipate problems, for even with the aid of clearer indicators such as costs, revenues and profits individual enterprises must look ahead. It simply means that town planning should concentrate on more modest, but more attainable, goals and become more successful and influential as a result.

SELECT BIBLIOGRAPHY

IT IS typical of town planning in Britain that although there are many *ad hoc* studies and articles on particular towns or aspects of planning, there are few *general* text-books, although J. B. Cullingworth's book (see below) is an excellent descriptive work. However, the following are suggested as general reading:

ANDERSON, M., *The Federal Bulldozer*, Massachusetts Institute of Technology Press, 1965.

BUCHANAN, C. D., *et alia, Traffic in Towns*, HMSO, 1963.

CULLINGWORTH, J. B., *Town and Country Planning in England and Wales*, Allen and Unwin, 1964.

FOLEY, D. L., *Controlling London's Growth*, University of California Press, 1963.

LICHFIELD, N., *Economics of Planned Development*, Estates Gazette, 1956.

LUTTRELL, W. F., *Factory Location and Industrial Movement*, National Institute of Economic and Social Research, 1962.

MANDELKER, D. R., *Green Belts and Urban Growth*, University of Wisconsin Press, 1962.

SELF, P., *Cities in Flood*, Faber, 1958.

STONE, P. A., *Housing, Town Development, Land and Costs*, Estates Gazette, 1963.

TURVEY, R., *The Economics of Real Property*, Allen and Unwin, 1957.

INDEX OF NAMES

INDEX OF SUBJECTS